The Villanova M
And 63 Other Dreams

A Game-by-Game Guide
To the 1985 NCAA Tournament

By

John Schaefer

Table of Contents

Table of Contents (continued)

Table of Contents (continued)

1984-85 Season in Review

A wave of change was sweeping over college basketball as the 1984-85 season dawned. Twenty-one conferences planned to use a 45-second shot clock (which would not be used in the NCAA tournament), and several leagues would continue to use variations of the 3-point line. Also, teams were given one extra timeout per game ("We'll need a guest speaker in the huddles," quipped Memphis State coach Dana Kirk) and coaches were now ordered to stay within a 28-foot-long box or risk being called for a technical foul ("We have to tippy-toe on the edge of the box," LSU's Dale Brown said. "It's like Korea, the 38th parallel").

But by far the biggest change had to do with the sport's marquee event – the NCAA tournament. The Big Dance, which invited just 32 teams as recently as 1978, expanded from 53 teams in 1984 to 64 for the '85 event, a decision that was supported by most coaches but was met with howls of protest from others who felt that the championship race was being watered down and the regular season made less meaningful.

"The coaches have been asking for this for some time," said Dave Gavitt, chairman of the tournament committee. "I think that every team that gets into the NCAA tournament wins." Michigan coach Bill Frieder said, "I like 64 teams because now everybody can play the same amount of games. I'd like to see it stay that way until the year 2000." Indiana's Bob Knight said he thought the 64-team field was "a logical number," although he warned that "I don't think there are 64 outstanding teams for the championship level." Sports Illustrated's Curry Kirkpatrick spoke for the dissenters when he wrote that the new "rainbow coalition NCAA tournament" was "dumb" and that "the tournament is so watered down now that even DePaul can get past the first round. But, sure, go ahead and open it up to everybody. Play the whole season for nothing."

While "change" was the watchword for the 1984-85 season, there was one overwhelming constant from the previous year – the Georgetown Hoyas. The defending champions were everyone's pick to become the first repeat winners since UCLA in 1973. With superstar center Patrick Ewing (who would go on to earn the Naismith Award as the national player of the year) intimidating foes with his shot-blocking prowess, a bevy of versatile and tenacious athletes and towering and glowering coach John Thompson orchestrating his special brand of "Hoya Paranoia", it's no wonder Oral Roberts coach Dick Acres called the championship fight "Georgetown and chase."

Even though the long campaign seemed like it would be just a formality before the Hoyas returned to their throne, there were several serious challengers poised to ascend to the top should Georgetown stumble. The Hoyas' Big East rival, St. John's, featured the crafty and deadly-accurate Chris Mullin. Memphis State (with Keith Lee and William Bedford) and Oklahoma (with two-time All-American Wayman Tisdale, who would enjoy a 55-point night against Texas State in December) had the big men who could dominate games just as well as Ewing. And defending Big Ten champ Illinois had a well-rounded and deep roster that played a brand of suffocating defense similar to Georgetown's.

While those teams largely lived up to expectations, there were several schools that thudded in 1984-85. At DePaul, coach Joey Meyer found that following in the footsteps of his legendary father Ray was a difficult task. The Blue Demons, who opened the season ranked No. 3, went into a tailspin after a 77-57 early-season drubbing at the hands of Georgetown and barely earned a spot in the expanded NCAA tourney field before being promptly dispatched by Syracuse in the opening round (and disproving Kirkpatrick's theory). Knight's Indiana team had high hopes thanks to its Elite Eight run in the '84 tournament and the presence of Steve Alford, who won an Olympic gold medal with his coach that summer. But the inexperienced Hoosiers struggled in the rugged Big Ten and Knight came under fire for his handling of the team, especially when he benched Alford for a game at Illinois and then heaved a chair across the court in anger during a defeat to Purdue.

UCLA, the team that would beat Indiana for the National Invitation Tournament title, was another college blueblood that had fallen on hard times. Under first-year head coach Walt Hazzard, the Bruins were 9-11 at one point before finishing the season strong and cutting down the nets at Madison Square Garden. Another of the NIT's final four, Louisville, saw its season ruined when senior Milt Wagner broke his foot in December and the team endured an embarrassing loss to little Chaminade in Hawaii. Denny Crum's Cardinals would rebound with a vengeance the following season, however, and win their second national title.

Georgetown dealt with few bumps on the road to Lexington, site of the 1985 Final Four. Before blasting DePaul, the Hoyas had annihilated UNLV 82-46 in Jerry Tarkanian's worst loss as Rebels coach. The Hoyas' record remained unblemished until a late January showdown with St. John's. The Redmen, who had been humiliated by tiny Niagara in December, ended the top-ranked Hoyas' 29-game winning streak with a thrilling 66-65 win to begin their own four-week run as the No. 1 team. Some said the Johnnies were aided by a lucky sweater that coach Lou Carnesecca first wore two weeks before the upset of Georgetown and had to plead with his wife to produce after she had hidden it because it was so ugly.

The Hoyas' only other regular-season loss came two days after the St. John's defeat when Syracuse beat them 65-63, meaning Georgetown was three points away from a perfect campaign. The Hoyas exacted revenge against the Redmen and reclaimed the top spot in the AP poll with an 85-69 romp on Feb. 27 (with Thompson drawing laughs by sporting a replica of Carnesecca's sweater) before closing out the season with another victory over St. John's in the Big East tournament final. The Big East rivals would be the only teams to be ranked No. 1 in 1984-85. Perhaps the biggest surprise of the season was Frieder's Michigan club. The Wolverines, who had not been to the NCAA tournament since 1977, ended that drought in a huge way by winning the Big Ten title and ending the season as the nation's second-ranked team.

College basketball was rocked by a scandal that erupted at Tulane at the end of the season. Several Green Wave players, including star forward John (Hot Rod) Williams, were implicated in a point-shaving scheme that cast a shadow over the Final Four. The players reportedly took $23,000 and cocaine to fix two games. The school responded to the scandal by abolishing its men's basketball program for four years.

The Final Four would serve as a showcase for the six-year-old Big East, which placed an unprecedented three of its members in the national semifinals. In three Elite Eight showdowns with the traditional basketball kingpin, the ACC, the youthful Big East handily won all three meetings, emphatically stating that there was a new power order in the world of college hoops. Georgetown and St. John's did not surprise anyone by making it to Lexington's Rupp Arena, but the third conference participant, Villanova, was the darling of the tournament, and in the final game of the season the Wildcats would spring one of the biggest surprises in basketball history.

Preseason Associated Press Top 20

1. Georgetown	11. UNLV
2. Illinois	12. Syracuse
3. DePaul	13. North Carolina State
4. Indiana	14. LSU
5. Oklahoma	15. Virginia Tech
6. Duke	16. Arkansas
7. St. John's	17. Louisville
8. Memphis State	18. Kentucky
9. Washington	19. Kansas
10. SMU	20. Georgia Tech

Final Associated Press Top 20

1. Georgetown	11. Virginia Commonwealth
2. Michigan	12. Illinois
3. St. John's	13. Kansas
4. Oklahoma	14. Loyola (IL)
5. Memphis State	15. Syracuse
6. Georgia Tech	16. North Carolina State
7. North Carolina	17. Texas Tech
8. Louisiana Tech	18. Tulsa
9. UNLV	19. Georgia
10. Duke	20. LSU and Michigan State (tied)

First Round

East Region
March 14
Hartford, CT
1. Georgetown 68
16. Lehigh 43

Few expected 12-18 Lehigh to force defending national champion and top-ranked Georgetown to even break a sweat. After all, the Engineers were a 33-point underdog. Comedian Bill Cosby told Lehigh coach Tom Schneider "to look ahead to finals – that is, final exams." Iowa coach George Raveling was less jovial, calling the Engineers' inclusion in the field of 64 "a farce."

That didn't stop Hoya coach John Thompson from expressing concern. "When people try and make me believe that something's going to come that easy, I get nervous – very nervous," he said.

In the end, Thompson had nothing to fear. The Hoyas scored eight seconds into the game and built a 39-11 halftime lead. Despite an off game from All-American center Patrick Ewing (3-of-9 shooting, 11 points, 4 rebounds), Georgetown still waltzed into the second round.

But Lehigh could take some satisfaction from the fact that it won the second half, 32-29. As Engineers point guard Mike Polaha, the game's leading scorer with 20 points, said of the Hoyas in a prophetic warning, "They are human. Very good humans, but humans."

	MIN	FGM-A	FTM-A	OFF	REB	AST	PF	PTS
Mike Androlewicz	20	1-6	0-0	1	2	3	0	2
Michael Polaha	39	9-17	2-2	0	1	1	1	20
Daren Queenan	35	2-12	9-10	4	7	2	2	13
Bill Cheslock	7	0-1	2-2	0	1	0	0	2
Erick Bronner	2	0-0	0-0	0	0	0	0	0
	MIN	FGM-A	FTM-A	OFF	REB	AST	PF	PTS
Gregory Martin	4	0-1	2-2	0	0	0	2	2
Tim Russell	26	0-2	0-0	0	4	1	2	0
Paul Wickman	10	0-1	0-0	0	2	0	5	0
Vernon Doswell	4	0-1	0-0	0	0	0	0	0
Ron Gregory	12	0-3	0-0	0	0	0	1	0
Seamus Dowling	9	0-0	0-0	0	1	0	2	0
Don Henderson	24	2-6	0-0	1	1	1	4	4
Victor McKay	1	0-0	0-0	0	0	0	1	0
Ken Greene	6	0-0	0-0	0	1	0	2	0

		FGM-A	FTM-A	OFF	REB	AST	PF	PTS
Joe McGarvey	1	0-0	0-0	0	0	0	0	0
TOTALS		FGM-A	FTM-A	OFF	REB	AST	PF	PTS
		14-50	15-16	6	20	8	22	43

GEORGETOWN HOYAS

	MIN	FGM-A	FTM-A	OFF	REB	AST	PF	PTS
Ralph Dalton	8	1-2	0-0	0	2	0	1	2
Reggie Williams	32	7-11	0-0	1	6	4	0	14
David Wingate	32	6-12	2-6	6	7	4	2	14
Kevin Floyd	4	0-0	0-0	0	1	1	0	0
Bill Martin	31	3-11	4-4	1	7	0	1	10
	MIN	FGM-A	FTM-A	OFF	REB	AST	PF	PTS
Grady Mateen	6	0-0	0-0	0	1	0	2	0
Perry McDonald	15	2-4	1-3	0	4	0	1	5
Ralph Highsmith	3	0-0	2-4	0	0	0	0	2
Tyrone Lockhart	1	0-0	0-0	0	0	0	0	0
Patrick Ewing	28	3-9	5-6	2	4	0	2	11
Horace Broadnax	19	0-2	0-0	0	5	4	4	0
Michael Jackson	21	4-6	2-2	0	1	3	4	10
TOTALS		FGM-A	FTM-A	OFF	REB	AST	PF	PTS
		26-57	16-25	10	38	16	17	68

8. Temple 60
9. Virginia Tech 57

Virginia Tech was rocked by dissension going into the tournament. Senior starters Perry Young (the Hokies' leading scorer and rebounder) and Tim Lewis were benched by coach Charlie Moir after they missed practice the day before the Temple game.

"If I had to make a decision right now, they wouldn't play at all," an angry Moir said. Young and Lewis were equally steamed, saying in a joint statement that they "did not realize we were practicing at that hour. Generally when a player is late, he gets a reminder by phone. We received no call."

Moir settled on a compromise, benching his two stars for the game's first 11 minutes. Predictably, Virginia Tech got off to a slow start. John Chaney's famed matchup zone gave the Hokies fits and the Owls ground out a 25-19 halftime lead. Lewis redeemed himself by sparking a second-half comeback. His layup with 5:50 left cut Temple's lead to 46-44, but Ed Coe sank a clutch jumper for the Owls and they sealed the victory from the foul line.

Young, for one, had no trouble pinning blame for the Hokies' loss. "It was a factor," Young said of Moir's decision to bench him and Lewis. "Temple was very beatable. It was bad timing and it had an effect on the whole team."

TEMPLE OWLS								
	MIN	FGM-A	FTM-A	OFF	REB	AST	PF	PTS
Tim Perry	11	0-0	0-0	1	1	0	2	0
Charles Rayne	40	3-9	6-8	4	10	3	2	12
Granger Hall	38	8-14	6-12	4	13	1	4	22
Ed Coe	35	3-8	4-8	1	6	2	2	10
Nate Blackwell	40	3-5	7-8	4	5	5	3	13
	MIN	FGM-A	FTM-A	OFF	REB	AST	PF	PTS
Derrick Brantley	7	0-0	0-0	0	0	0	1	0
Howard Evans	29	1-4	1-3	1	2	2	2	3
TOTALS		FGM-A	FTM-A	OFF	REB	AST	PF	PTS
		18-40	24-39	15	37	13	16	60

	MIN	FGM-A	FTM-A	OFF	REB	AST	PF	PTS
Perry Young	29	4-14	2-5	3	5	1	4	10
Bobby Beecher	16	4-5	0-1	2	2	0	5	8
Keith Colbert	36	3-8	5-8	3	10	3	5	11
Dell Curry	37	6-14	1-1	1	3	5	5	13
Dave Burgess	22	1-2	1-1	0	2	0	3	3
	MIN	FGM-A	FTM-A	OFF	REB	AST	PF	PTS
Ron Everhart	18	2-4	0-0	1	2	0	0	4
Phil Williams	16	1-1	0-0	1	3	1	1	2
Tim Lewis	26	3-10	0-1	1	1	1	2	6
TOTALS		FGM-A	FTM-A	OFF	REB	AST	PF	PTS
		24-58	9-17	12	28	11	25	57

5. SMU 85

12. Old Dominion 68

"I'm ready to play somebody different, and I think the rest of the guys are, too," said SMU big man Jon Koncak. "We need some fresh air."

Koncak's sentiment was understandable since the Mustangs, after a 16-0 start to the season and a ranking as high as No. 2 in the nation, lost 9 of their final 16 games. But Old Dominion would prove to be a big breath of fresh air.

Mark Davis was a one-man army for the Monarchs, scoring a game-high 32 points, but he alone could not thwart SMU's balanced attack – Carl Wright scored 18 points and Koncak and Larry Davis added 17 each. The Mustangs methodically built an 8-point halftime lead and then poured it on in the second half, shooting a blistering 59 percent for the game. The rout only served to raise questions over why Old Dominion, 18-11 and third in the mediocre Sun Belt Conference, got an at-large bid in the first place.

SOUTHERN METHODIST MUSTANGS

	MIN	FGM-A	FTM-A	OFF	REB	AST	PF	PTS
Reginald Pink	4	0-0	0-0	0	2	0	1	0
Glen Puddy	1	0-0	0-0	0	0	0	0	0
Terry Thomas	1	0-0	0-0	0	0	0	0	0
Terry Williams	14	7-7	1-2	1	6	0	1	15
Coyle Winborn	1	0-0	0-0	0	0	0	0	0
	MIN	FGM-A	FTM-A	OFF	REB	AST	PF	PTS
Carl Wright	34	8-16	2-2	0	3	7	1	18
Alan Cozart	1	0-0	0-0	0	0	0	0	0
Johnny Fuller	3	0-0	0-0	0	0	0	0	0
Kevin Lewis	21	1-3	0-0	0	2	1	2	2
Scott Johnson	21	0-2	2-2	0	0	1	1	2
Jon Koncak	27	8-14	1-6	6	11	1	4	17
Larry Davis	37	8-14	1-1	5	15	2	1	17
Butch Moore	34	6-8	2-4	0	2	10	2	14
John Briggs	1	0-0	0-0	0	1	0	0	0
TOTALS		FGM-A	FTM-A	OFF	REB	AST	PF	PTS
		38-64	9-17	12	42	22	13	85

OLD DOMINION MONARCHS

	MIN	FGM-A	FTM-A	OFF	REB	AST	PF	PTS
Keith Thomas	24	2-13	0-0	4	5	1	2	4
Clarence Hanley	21	2-6	1-2	1	3	1	4	5
Ronnie Wade	4	0-0	0-1	0	0	0	1	0
Steve Trax	1	0-1	0-0	0	0	0	0	0
Sylvester Charles	20	2-5	0-0	1	2	1	0	4
	MIN	FGM-A	FTM-A	OFF	REB	AST	PF	PTS
Darryl Tolson	1	0-0	0-0	0	0	0	0	0
Matt White	1	0-0	0-0	0	0	0	0	0
Charlie Smith	17	4-9	1-2	0	2	2	0	9
Frank Smith	37	1-5	1-2	0	1	8	1	3

Fred Facka	1	0-0	0-0	0	0	0	0	0
Horace Lambert	6	0-1	0-0	0	1	2	2	0
Kenny Gattison	32	5-15	1-2	5	10	2	4	11
Mark Davis	35	14-22	4-4	5	10	3	4	32
TOTALS		FGM-A	FTM-A	OFF	REB	AST	PF	PTS
		30-77	8-13	16	34	20	18	68

4. Loyola (IL) 59
13. Iona 58

The situation was eerily similar for Iona: a chance to tie up a first-round NCAA tournament game from the free throw line in the closing seconds. Just one year earlier Rory Grimes failed in the clutch with two seconds left as the Gaels lost a heartbreaker to Virginia.

Now it was Tony Hargraves' turn. Just like Grimes, Hargraves made the first of a one-and-one, this time with three seconds on the clock. After Loyola called a timeout to ice him, Hargraves sent Iona to another bitter defeat as his second attempt clanged off the front of the rim.

"I was in the same situation last year," Grimes mused. "I can sympathize with him."

Loyola, which extended its nation's-best winning streak to 18 games, was paced as usual by superstar Alfredrick Hughes. The NCAA's leading scorer at 27.4 points per game poured in 24 and passed Elvin Hayes for fifth place on the all-time scoring list with 2,892 points.

IONA GAELS							
	FGM-A	FTM-A	OFF	REB	AST	PF	PTS
Tony Hargraves	9-16	1-7	-	7	0	3	19
Troy Truesdale	1-2	4-5	-	8	2	4	6
Bob Coleman	6-11	2-3	-	16	0	2	14
Wendall Walters	0-0	0-0	-	1	0	0	0
Richie Simmonds	0-3	1-2	-	0	1	0	1
	FGM-A	FTM-A	OFF	REB	AST	PF	PTS
Rory Grimes	5-13	0-1	-	1	7	4	10
John Kijonik	2-3	4-4	-	3	1	2	8
Arnie Russell	0-3	0-0	-	1	0	2	0
TOTALS	FGM-A	FTM-A	OFF	REB	AST	PF	PTS
	23-51	12-22	-	37	11	17	58

LOYOLA (IL) RAMBLERS							
	FGM-A	FTM-A	OFF	REB	AST	PF	PTS
Ivan Young	0-0	0-1	-	1	0	3	0

	FGM-A	FTM-A	OFF	REB	AST	PF	PTS
Andre Battle	7-18	1-2	-	6	2	3	15
Mike Cenar	0-1	0-0	-	1	0	1	0
Greg Williams	1-2	2-2	-	6	2	3	4
Carl Golston	3-8	2-3	-	0	12	2	8
	FGM-A	FTM-A	OFF	REB	AST	PF	PTS
Andre Moore	4-6	0-0	-	5	0	5	8
Alfredrick Hughes	10-23	4-7	-	11	1	3	24
TOTALS	FGM-A	FTM-A	OFF	REB	AST	PF	PTS
	25-58	9-15	-	30	17	20	59

March 15

Atlanta

6. Georgia 67

11. Wichita State 59

Going into its opener, Georgia had only two words on its mind: Xavier McDaniel. Wichita State's "X-Man", after all, was an All-American and perhaps the most productive player in the country, as he led in both scoring (27.4 points per game, tied with Loyola's Alfredrick Hughes) and rebounding (15 per game).

"We're not going to stop him," Bulldogs coach Hugh Durham predicted. "We just don't want him to get 50."

McDaniel didn't even get half that amount, finishing with 22 points. But he was all-too unstoppable in the first half. The Shocker great's 18 points helped his team go into the locker room tied at 27.

Georgia's swarming, high-pressure defense kicked into gear in the second half and limited McDaniel to just 4 points. He was effectively neutralized by the Bulldogs' star freshman center, Cedric Henderson, who scored 20 to lead a typically balanced Dawg attack before a partisan crowd in Atlanta. A 16-2 Georgia run midway through the half proved to be decisive.

WICHITA STATE SHOCKERS								
	MIN	FGM-A	FTM-A	OFF	REB	AST	PF	PTS
Curtis Bailey	2	0-0	0-0	-	1	0	1	0
Mike Arline	31	1-7	1-2	-	0	3	1	3
Karl Papke	22	5-10	1-1	-	5	2	4	11
Henry Carr	26	1-3	0-0	-	4	0	3	2
Clint Normore	9	0-1	0-0	-	0	0	0	0
	MIN	FGM-A	FTM-A	OFF	REB	AST	PF	PTS
Cedric Coleman	32	2-3	0-2	-	8	2	1	4
Aubrey Sherrod	40	8-16	1-1	-	3	1	4	17
Xavier McDaniel	37	11-18	0-0	-	11	0	5	22

	MIN	FGM-A	FTM-A	OFF	REB	AST	PF	PTS
Tom Kosich	1	0-0	0-0	-	0	0	0	0
TOTALS		FGM-A	FTM-A	OFF	REB	AST	PF	PTS
		28-58	3-6	-	32	8	19	59

GEORGIA BULLDOGS								
	MIN	FGM-A	FTM-A	OFF	REB	AST	PF	PTS
Joe Ward	23	5-10	0-0	-	5	1	2	10
Richard Corhen	24	2-5	3-4	-	6	1	1	7
Gerald Crosby	31	5-8	3-4	-	2	5	1	13
Chad Kessler	9	0-0	1-3	-	1	0	0	1
Melvin Howard	15	2-3	2-4	-	1	1	0	6
	MIN	FGM-A	FTM-A	OFF	REB	AST	PF	PTS
Donald Hartry	34	2-7	0-0	-	4	3	0	4
David Dunn	16	0-3	0-0	-	6	0	0	0
Cedric Henderson	24	10-18	0-2	-	6	2	4	20
Horace McMillan	24	3-3	0-0	-	2	3	2	6
TOTALS		FGM-A	FTM-A	OFF	REB	AST	PF	PTS
		29-57	9-17	-	33	16	10	67

3. Illinois 76
14. Northeastern 57

Jim Calhoun would have better days in the NCAA tournament.

The two-time national champion at UConn was still an up-and-comer when he and superstar Reggie Lewis faced the rugged Illini. Illinois never trailed in the game, led by 12 points at halftime and built a 29-point edge in the second half while coasting into the second round.

Lewis, as usual, was the focus of the Huskies' attack, jacking up almost half of his team's shots (28 of 58) while scoring 22 points, including 8 in the final 3:30 as Northeastern made the final score more respectable.

Ken "Snake" Norman continued his emergence for Illinois. The sophomore center entered the starting lineup two weeks earlier because of injuries and quickly stamped himself as the Illini's most dangerous offensive player. He feasted on the Huskies for a game-high 23 points on 8-of-11 shooting.

NORTHEASTERN HUSKIES								
	MIN	FGM-A	FTM-A	OFF	REB	AST	PF	PTS
Quinton Dale	33	4-10	2-2	-	7	0	4	10
John Williams	24	4-6	1-4	-	1	3	5	9
Gerald Corcoran	5	1-1	0-0	-	2	0	1	2

	MIN	FGM-A	FTM-A	OFF	REB	AST	PF	PTS
Wes Fuller	25	0-0	0-0	-	4	0	1	0
Ernie McDonald	8	1-2	0-0	-	0	0	1	2
	MIN	FGM-A	FTM-A	OFF	REB	AST	PF	PTS
Kevin McDuffie	29	2-3	2-4	-	5	0	2	6
Steve Evans	4	0-2	0-0	-	0	0	0	0
Reggie Lewis	34	11-28	0-0	-	5	1	3	22
Andre Lafleur	38	3-6	0-0	-	1	7	2	6
TOTALS		FGM-A	FTM-A	OFF	REB	AST	PF	PTS
		26-58	5-10	-	25	11	19	57

ILLINOIS FIGHTING ILLINI

	MIN	FGM-A	FTM-A	OFF	REB	AST	PF	PTS
Scott Haffner	6	0-2	1-2	-	3	0	0	1
Doug Altenberger	30	6-10	1-2	-	3	2	2	13
Ken Norman	33	8-11	7-7	-	9	4	1	23
Anthony Welch	25	6-11	1-2	-	2	2	2	13
Efrem Winters	31	4-5	3-4	-	7	4	1	11
	MIN	FGM-A	FTM-A	OFF	REB	AST	PF	PTS
Reggie Woodward	4	1-1	0-0	-	0	1	2	2
Tony Wysinger	23	2-4	2-2	-	3	2	2	6
Bruce Douglas	32	1-5	1-2	-	4	4	2	3
Scott Meents	16	2-3	0-1	-	1	2	1	4
TOTALS		FGM-A	FTM-A	OFF	REB	AST	PF	PTS
		30-52	16-22	-	32	21	13	76

7. Syracuse 70
10. DePaul 65

Rony Seikaly was still a little-known big man from Greece when he took his initial step on the NCAA tournament stage. When the night ended, he had his first starring role.

The freshman scored 17 points, 9 above his season average, and added 9 rebounds as 15th-ranked Syracuse advanced. "No question he was the difference," Orangemen coach Jim Boeheim said. "Especially in the first half when he had 12 points."

Syracuse was paced by magnificent point guard Dwayne "Pearl" Washington, who was the game's leading scorer with 23 points, including 15-of-16 from the foul line. That helped offset a poor night from the team's top scorer, Rafael Addison, who shot only 2 of 13 while being held to 8 points. Boeheim's notorious zone defense held DePaul to 43 percent shooting.

Blue Demons coach Joey Meyer didn't just inherit the DePaul program from his legendary father Ray, he also continued his dad's knack for flopping in the Big Dance. The Orangemen took the lead for good with 7:51 left in the first half and built its largest lead of 10 points early in the second half. They then had to withstand several Blue Demon rallies, including a chance in the final minute to cut the deficit to two when Kevin Holmes seemed to have a steal. But he couldn't get a handle of the ball and lost it out of bounds, along with DePaul's hopes for a win.

"That's the way our season went, we either fumbled it or missed it," lamented Meyer.

DEPAUL BLUE DEMONS

	MIN	FGM-A	FTM-A	OFF	REB	AST	PF	PTS
Kenny Patterson	40	5-13	1-1	-	4	15	4	11
Randy Pettus	1	0-0	0-0	-	0	0	0	0
Lawrence West	31	4-11	1-2	-	3	3	5	9
Dallas Comegys	35	5-15	5-7	-	10	1	1	15
Tyrone Corbin	40	7-14	3-6	-	8	1	4	17
	MIN	FGM-A	FTM-A	OFF	REB	AST	PF	PTS
Kevin Holmes	15	0-0	0-0	-	2	0	3	0
Marty Embry	23	5-6	2-2	-	2	0	5	12
Lemone Lampley	6	0-0	0-0	-	0	0	0	0
Tony Jackson	9	0-2	1-2	-	1	0	2	1
TOTALS		FGM-A	FTM-A	OFF	REB	AST	PF	PTS
		26-61	13-20	-	30	20	24	65

SYRACUSE ORANGEMEN

	MIN	FGM-A	FTM-A	OFF	REB	AST	PF	PTS
Rafael Addison	40	2-13	4-4	-	9	3	4	8
Wendell Alexis	27	3-3	3-4	-	5	4	4	9
Dwayne Washington	40	4-8	15-16	-	3	4	1	23
Herman Harried	8	1-3	0-0	-	2	0	1	2
Rony Seikaly	29	7-9	3-4	-	9	0	4	17
	MIN	FGM-A	FTM-A	OFF	REB	AST	PF	PTS
Melvin Brown	11	1-2	0-0	-	0	0	2	2
Andre Hawkins	17	0-2	1-3	-	4	0	1	1
Greg Monroe	28	4-6	0-1	-	2	2	0	8
TOTALS		FGM-A	FTM-A	OFF	REB	AST	PF	PTS
		22-46	26-32	-	34	13	17	70

2. Georgia Tech 65
15. Mercer 58

A funny thing happened on the way to a rout. Georgia Tech was expected to waltz in its first trip to the Big Dance since 1960 and that's just what the Yellow Jackets were doing at the outset, amassing an 18-point lead that carried into the second half.

But then Tech, which perhaps had trouble coming off the high of its first ACC championship, got sloppy, especially from the foul line, as the Bears crept within six points in the closing minutes. Even the normally dead-eye Mark Price missed four of his eight charity attempts, and the huge contingent of Jacket fans in Atlanta feared their team might blow its first NCAA tournament win in a quarter century.

In the end, the dominating presence of 6-11 center Yvon Joseph proved too much for Mercer to overcome. Joseph was most effective in Georgia Tech's big first half and finished with 19 points, more than offsetting the 17 scored by Mercer star and future NBA Coach of the Year Sam Mitchell.

Tech coach Bobby Cremins was so upset with his team's performance that he called a 2 AM film session to review the game. "I told them, 'If we're gonna play like this against Syracuse (Tech's second-round opponent), let me know because I'll go recruiting,'" he said.

MERCER BEARS

	MIN	FGM-A	FTM-A	OFF	REB	AST	PF	PTS
Earl Walker	39	8-20	1-2	-	14	2	2	17
Eric Chambers	1	0-0	0-0	-	0	0	0	0
Elston Harris	18	0-0	0-0	-	0	4	4	0
Keith Czapla	23	0-2	0-1	-	3	4	4	0
Sam Mitchell	40	5-16	7-8	-	6	0	4	17
	MIN	FGM-A	FTM-A	OFF	REB	AST	PF	PTS
Pete Geter	14	0-3	0-0	-	2	1	2	0
Chris Moore	23	1-6	1-3	-	6	0	5	3
Doug Guthrie	12	1-2	2-2	-	3	0	3	4
TOTALS		FGM-A	FTM-A	OFF	REB	AST	PF	PTS
		15-49	11-16	-	34	11	24	41

GEORGIA TECH YELLOW JACKETS

	MIN	FGM-A	FTM-A	OFF	REB	AST	PF	PTS
Scott Petway	40	3-5	1-3	-	3	4	4	7
Mark Price	40	5-13	4-8	-	2	4	2	14
Henry Dalrymple	37	3-11	7-8	-	11	4	4	13
John Salley	28	2-4	4-8	-	7	2	3	8
Antoine Ford	10	2-4	0-0	-	3	1	2	4
	MIN	FGM-A	FTM-A	OFF	REB	AST	PF	PTS

John Martinson	3	0-0	0-0	-	0	1	0	0
Jack Mansell	6	0-0	0-0	-	2	0	0	0
Yvon Joseph	36	8-13	3-4	-	9	0	3	19
TOTALS		FGM-A	FTM-A	OFF	REB	AST	PF	PTS
		23-50	19-31	-	37	16	18	65

West Region

March 14
Salt Lake City, UT
1. St. John's 83
16. Southern 59

In his 17th season as St. John's coach, lovable Lou Carnesecca and his latest lucky sweater headed out West in search of his first trip to the Final Four. Carnesecca debuted a sweater that had snowflakes on it, saying, "This is my sweater for the tournament. I think it's kind of apropos for this area. When in Rome, do as the Romans do."

The Redmen seemed pleased to be sent out to low-key Salt Lake City, even if they needed to enlist the University of Utah band to fill in for their own. "In New York, you couldn't turn around without somebody being in your pocket," Carnesecca complained.

Undersized Southern needed some magic of its own against the star-studded Redmen. The Jaguars didn't get it. Chris Mullin, Bill Wennington and Walter Berry all shot better than 50 percent and scored more than 20 points each in the rout. Wennington used his 7-foot frame to net seven quick points as third-ranked St. John's jumped to a 34-18 halftime lead and cruised from there.

Carnesecca lauded his team's defense, which he said "was the best we've played in quite a while." Southern coach Bob Hopkins, meanwhile, had little to offer in the way of analysis. "How can I say anything about their weaknesses when they just kicked my fanny," he asked.

ST. JOHN'S REDMEN	MIN	FGM-A	FTM-A	OFF	REB	AST	PF	PTS
Bill Wennington	36	10-12	3-5	-	8	5	3	23
Steve Shurina	1	0-0	0-0	-	0	0	0	0
Ron Stewart	15	0-0	0-1	-	0	0	2	0
Walter Berry	34	9-17	6-7	-	13	1	2	24
Ron Rowan	3	0-0	0-0	-	0	0	0	0
	MIN	FGM-A	FTM-A	OFF	REB	AST	PF	PTS
Terry Bross	1	1-1	0-0	-	0	0	1	2
Mike Moses	23	0-2	3-5	-	0	3	3	3
Chris Mullin	36	7-12	7-10	-	4	6	2	21

	MIN	FGM-A	FTM-A	OFF	REB	AST	PF	PTS
Mark Jackson	17	1-4	2-2	-	3	2	2	4
Shelton Jones	7	1-1	0-0	-	3	0	2	2
Willie Glass	27	1-2	2-2	-	6	2	1	4
TOTALS		FGM-A	FTM-A	OFF	REB	AST	PF	PTS
		30-51	23-32	-	37	19	18	83

SOUTHERN JAGUARS								
	MIN	FGM-A	FTM-A	OFF	REB	AST	PF	PTS
Jones Kelly	1	0-1	0-0	-	0	0	0	0
Glenn Dedmon	39	4-10	4-5	-	5	5	2	12
Byron Gabriel	39	5-13	3-3	-	2	4	3	13
Donevin Hoskins	39	6-12	5-6	-	5	0	4	17
James Faulkner	1	0-1	0-0	-	0	0	0	0
	MIN	FGM-A	FTM-A	OFF	REB	AST	PF	PTS
Jeff Faulkner	21	2-4	1-4	-	2	1	3	5
James Lee	32	5-14	0-0	-	5	0	4	10
Lloyd Legarde	1	1-1	0-0	-	1	0	0	2
David Ponton	6	0-0	0-3	-	0	0	0	0
John Staves	13	0-2	0-0	-	3	0	5	0
Bridges	7	0-2	0-0	-	0	0	1	0
TOTALS		FGM-A	FTM-A	OFF	REB	AST	PF	PTS
		23-60	13-21	-	23	10	22	59

9. Arkansas 63
8. Iowa 54

Iowa can be forgiven if it was feeling overly confident. The Hawkeyes, after all, had handed Eddie Sutton his second-worst defeat ever at Arkansas earlier in the season, a 71-52 drubbing. But the fact that Iowa had lost six of its previous eight games probably gave a better indication of how the rematch would go.

The first half picked up where their last meeting had left off as the hot-shooting Hawkeyes held a 33-26 lead into the locker room. Then Joe Kleine took over. The Razorbacks center, who had won Olympic gold the previous summer, scored 15 of his 25 points in the second half to go with his 14 rebounds while Iowa's shooting touch suddenly disappeared. The Hawkeyes made only 31 percent of their shots in the final 20 minutes, and only 6 of their 15 free throws for the game.

"I tried not to think about Kleine before the game," Iowa coach George Raveling admitted. "If I had, only me and my laundry man would have known how afraid I was."

Kleine keyed an eight-point run that gave Arkansas a 52-44 lead and the Hogs were never threatened the rest of the way. Iowa's top player and all-time leading scorer, Greg Stokes, was thoroughly dominated in his individual battle with Kleine, finishing with just 14 points before fouling out.

The Razorbacks refused to let speculation about Sutton's future distract them. Sutton had said before the game that he would be at Arkansas for many more years, even though Auburn Athletic Director Pat Dye claimed that Sutton had inquired about that school's vacant coaching position.

IOWA HAWKEYES

	MIN	FGM-A	FTM-A	OFF	REB	AST	PF	PTS
Andre Banks	35	3-8	0-1	-	5	6	3	6
Michael Payne	33	1-4	0-0	-	4	1	2	2
Michael Reaves	8	0-2	0-0	-	0	1	1	0
Gerry Wright	25	5-7	4-7	-	5	2	3	14
Dave Snedeker	3	0-0	0-0	-	1	0	1	0
	MIN	FGM-A	FTM-A	OFF	REB	AST	PF	PTS
Greg Stokes	32	6-12	2-2	-	8	2	5	14
Todd Berkenpas	31	8-17	0-1	-	2	2	3	16
Kent Hill	1	0-0	0-0	-	0	1	1	0
Jeff Moe	7	0-2	0-0	-	0	2	0	0
Bill Jones	3	0-1	0-2	-	1	1	2	0
Al Lorenzen	21	1-3	0-2	-	3	0	3	2
Michael Morgan	1	0-1	0-0	-	0	0	0	0
TOTALS		FGM-A	FTM-A	OFF	REB	AST	PF	PTS
		24-57	6-15	-	29	18	24	54

	MIN	FGM-A	FTM-A	OFF	REB	AST	PF	PTS
Charles Balentine	39	6-7	2-2	-	8	3	4	14
Byron Irvin	14	1-6	0-0	-	1	0	0	2
Eric Poerschke	1	0-0	0-0	-	0	0	0	0
Kevin Rehl	6	1-2	0-0	-	0	1	2	2
William Mills	27	2-6	6-8	-	3	5	4	10
	MIN	FGM-A	FTM-A	OFF	REB	AST	PF	PTS
Allie. Freeman	28	3-5	0-0	-	4	2	0	6
Joe Kleine	38	10-17	5-8	-	14	0	3	25
Andrew Lang	8	0-0	0-2	-	0	0	2	0
Stephen Moore	9	0-0	0-0	-	1	0	0	0
Kenny Hutchinson	30	0-3	4-7	-	3	5	3	4
TOTALS		FGM-A	FTM-A	OFF	REB	AST	PF	PTS

23-46	17-27	-	34	16	18	63	

12. Kentucky 66
5. Washington 58

Arkansas' Eddie Sutton wasn't the only coach whose future was a hot topic in Salt Lake City. Kentucky's Joe B. Hall was facing the latest round of speculation that he would either quit or be fired, while Washington's Marv Harshman had already announced that he was retiring after 40 seasons.

An even bigger storyline for this game was Kentucky's mere presence. Probably no team benefitted more from the tournament's expansion to 64 teams than 16-12 Kentucky, whose inclusion created an uproar. "A lot of people question us being here," said Hall. "That is a motivating factor, and we're going to play well."

Thanks to superstar Kenny Walker's double-double (29 points, 10 rebounds and a resounding shot block against future NFL draft bust Reggie Rogers), the Wildcats silenced their critics. But the Huskies came tantalizingly close to topping the 'Cats. Eight times in the second half Washington crept within a point, but the Pac-10 co-champs could never take the lead.

The Huskies got their usual all-around excellent game from Detlef Schrempf (16 points, 7 rebounds, 5 assists), but it wasn't enough to extend Harshman's career one more game. "I just told them thanks," he said later, while Schrempf recalled, "It was pretty emotional in the locker room."

KENTUCKY WILDCATS

	MIN	FGM-A	FTM-A	OFF	REB	AST	PF	PTS
Bret Bearup	-	1-5	5-6	-	6	2	5	7
Kenny Walker	-	8-15	13-15	-	10	1	3	29
Roger Harden	-	1-5	2-4	-	3	4	2	4
Winston Bennett	-	1-5	1-2	-	2	2	2	3
Ed Davender	-	2-8	5-7	-	4	3	1	9
	MIN	FGM-A	FTM-A	OFF	REB	AST	PF	PTS
Richard Madison	-	3-3	4-4	-	3	0	1	10
Troy McKinley	-	1-1	0-0	-	0	0	0	2
James Blackmon	-	1-3	0-2	-	3	0	1	2
Cedric Jenkins	-	0-2	0-0	-	2	0	2	0
Robert Lock	-	0-0	0-0	-	3	0	0	0
TOTALS		FGM-A	FTM-A	OFF	REB	AST	PF	PTS
		18-47	30-40	-	36	12	17	66

WASHINGTON HUSKIES

MIN	FGM-A	FTM-A	OFF	REB	AST	PF	PTS

	MIN	FGM-A	FTM-A	OFF	REB	AST	PF	PTS
J.D. Taylor	1	0-0	0-0	-	0	0	1	0
Clay Damon	24	2-5	0-0	-	2	4	5	4
Chris Welp	34	4-11	2-2	-	9	0	4	10
Shag Williams	35	4-8	0-0	-	7	0	3	8
David Wilson	1	0-0	0-0	-	0	0	0	0
	MIN	FGM-A	FTM-A	OFF	REB	AST	PF	PTS
Kevin Vidato	7	1-2	0-0	-	1	1	1	2
Detlef Schrempf	40	7-11	2-5	-	7	5	4	16
Reggie Rogers	5	1-2	0-0	-	0	0	2	2
Paul Fortier	36	7-14	2-8	-	6	4	4	16
Tony Morrell	17	0-2	0-1	-	1	1	4	0
TOTALS		FGM-A	FTM-A	OFF	REB	AST	PF	PTS
		26-55	6-16	-	33	15	28	58

4. UNLV 85
13. San Diego State 80

The shot clock still wasn't in use in the NCAA tournament, but even if it was it could have been left off for this high-octane matchup. "We're going to run," UNLV coach Jerry Tarkanian promised. "We're not going to change our game."

The ninth-ranked Rebels entered the tournament on a roll, winning 26 of 27 games since being destroyed at Georgetown by 36 points in December. But the talk before the game wasn't about UNLV's standing as the best team in the West but rather about how the school had been denied admission to San Diego State's Western Athletic Conference five years earlier.

"That's the best thing that ever happened to us," Tarkanian said of that decision, but he refused to admit that he felt extra motivation to defeat the WAC champion.

UNLV seemed to be in trouble early when its leading scorer and rebounder, Richie Adams, picked up his third foul just six minutes into the game. But the Rebels went on a run led by Armon Gilliam and Anthony Jones as Adams sat sulking on the bench, and they took a 43-33 lead at halftime.

Tarkanian had been unusually relaxed until this point. That would change in the second half as the Aztecs made their move, pulling even at 56 with 10 minutes left and prompting Tark the Shark to start chomping on his famed towel. UNLV snapped out of its funk, however, when Adams finally started playing like the conference player of the year that he was, scoring four quick points to give his team a lead it would never surrender.

SAN DIEGO STATE AZTECS								
	MIN	FGM-A	FTM-A	OFF	REB	AST	PF	PTS
Leonard Allen	36	8-10	7-10	-	9	0	4	23

	MIN	FGM-A	FTM-A	OFF	REB	AST	PF	PTS
Anthony Watson	33	9-15	1-4	-	3	6	5	19
Andre Ross	8	2-4	1-1	-	3	0	1	5
John Martens	28	4-8	3-4	-	2	0	4	11
Jeff Konek	20	1-5	3-4	-	3	7	4	5
	MIN	FGM-A	FTM-A	OFF	REB	AST	PF	PTS
Creon Dorsey	31	0-3	2-4	-	6	8	3	2
Gerald Murray	7	0-0	0-0	-	0	0	1	0
Bobbie Owens	8	2-3	0-0	-	0	0	0	4
TOTALS		FGM-A	FTM-A	OFF	REB	AST	PF	PTS
		26-48	17-27	-	26	21	22	69

UNLV REBELS

	MIN	FGM-A	FTM-A	OFF	REB	AST	PF	PTS
Richie Adams	23	4-11	2-2	-	4	0	4	10
Freddie Banks	31	2-7	4-5	-	5	8	1	8
Ed Catchings	15	2-4	4-4	-	3	1	2	8
Richard Robinson	20	3-7	0-0	-	2	0	5	6
Anthony Jones	34	9-13	0-1	-	4	4	3	18
	MIN	FGM-A	FTM-A	OFF	REB	AST	PF	PTS
Frank James	27	3-8	4-4	-	2	4	3	10
Armon Gilliam	31	7-12	7-12	-	10	2	2	21
Gary Graham	13	1-3	0-0	-	0	3	2	2
Eldridge Hudson	6	1-2	0-0	-	1	1	2	2
TOTALS		FGM-A	FTM-A	OFF	REB	AST	PF	PTS
		32-67	21-28	-	31	23	24	85

March 15

Albuquerque, NM

11. UTEP 79

6. Tulsa 75

Chalk one up for the teacher. In a matchup featuring legendary coach Don Haskins and one of his pupils, Nolan Richardson, the Miners recorded an upset win, but not before enduring a near-epic collapse.

Texas-El Paso held an eight-point lead over 18th-ranked Tulsa with 1:17 remaining when the Golden Hurricane stormed back. They trimmed the deficit to two and had a shot at tying the game in the closing seconds. But David Moss' 10-foot jumper was off the mark, UTEP's Dave Feitl grabbed the rebound and then made two free throws to finally secure Haskins' first NCAA tournament win in 18 years.

Long before it was labeled "Forty Minutes of Hell", Richardson's famed full-court pressing attack was perhaps too aggressive on this day. The Hurricane were whistled for 34 fouls that handed the Miners a whopping 55 free throw attempts, of which they made 39. That helped UTEP overcome the offensive outburst of Tulsa guard Steve Harris, who lit up the Miners for 31 points.

Years later, after Haskins had died in 2008, Richardson made it clear just how special "The Bear" was to him. "What you saw was what you got," Richardson said of Haskins, for whom he played for two years at UTEP when it was known as Texas Western. "And I loved that so much. I tried to emulate that in my career. The championship we won (at Arkansas in 1994) ... it all came from The Bear."

UTEP MINERS								
	MIN	FGM-A	FTM-A	OFF	REB	AST	PF	PTS
Donnell Allen	13	0-1	0-2	-	3	0	1	0
Kevin Hamilton	27	0-1	2-5	-	6	1	3	2
Jamaal Smith	30	4-6	5-6	-	3	2	5	13
Quintan Gates	16	1-1	1-2	-	1	0	4	3
Dave Feitl	30	4-11	9-12	-	9	0	2	17
	MIN	FGM-A	FTM-A	OFF	REB	AST	PF	PTS
Kent Lockhart	33	4-8	8-10	-	2	3	5	16
Jeep Jackson	12	0-1	5-8	-	1	1	1	5
Luster Goodwin	39	7-13	9-10	-	5	0	3	23
TOTALS		FGM-A	FTM-A	OFF	REB	AST	PF	PTS
		20-42	39-55	-	30	7	24	79

TULSA GOLDEN HURRICANE								
	MIN	FGM-A	FTM-A	OFF	REB	AST	PF	PTS
Jeff Rahilly	3	0-1	0-0	-	0	1	0	0
Vince Williams	22	3-3	2-3	-	2	0	5	8
Steve Harris	39	12-22	7-8	-	5	2	5	31
Herb Suggs	2	0-0	0-0	-	0	0	2	0
Anthony Fobbs	12	0-0	0-1	-	2	0	4	0
	MIN	FGM-A	FTM-A	OFF	REB	AST	PF	PTS
Carlton McKinney	7	0-1	0-0	-	0	0	1	0
Byron Boudreaux	22	2-5	0-0	-	0	2	3	4
Clifford Langford	4	0-0	0-0	-	1	0	3	0
David Moss	31	5-9	2-2	-	6	0	4	12
Herbert Johnson	39	4-12	2-3	-	8	2	3	10
Tracy Moore	19	3-6	4-4	-	1	1	4	10
TOTALS		FGM-A	FTM-A	OFF	REB	AST	PF	PTS
		29-59	17-21	-	25	8	34	75

3. North Carolina State 65
14. Nevada 56

Call it a coincidence, an omen or a calculated decision by the tournament selection committee. Whatever the forces that made it happen, Jim Valvano was just happy to call "The Pit" home again.

The North Carolina State coach was practically giddy to return to the site of his team's monumental upset of Houston for the 1983 championship in the Wolfpack's last NCAA tournament game. He knelt and kissed the ground when he arrived in Albuquerque. "It was unrehearsed," Jimmy V claimed. "I cut my lip."

Lorenzo Charles then got busy shredding the "other" Wolf Pack. The man who slammed home the winning points in the '83 final picked up where he left off in New Mexico, dominating Nevada in the paint with 22 points and 12 rebounds. "I have seen him more explosive," Valvano said of his senior. "Of course, I always expect great things of him."

The Wolfpack struggled with Nevada's zone defense before turning to their inside muscle to build a 14-point second-half advantage. The Wolf Pack cut the deficit to six with 6:40 left before N.C. State went on one final run and then used a delay game to chew up the clock.

NEVADA WOLF PACK

	MIN	FGM-A	FTM-A	OFF	REB	AST	PF	PTS
Dwayne Randall	36	6-13	2-2	-	9	0	3	14
Mike Parillo	11	1-5	0-0	-	1	0	1	2
Ed Porter	21	0-1	1-2	-	3	0	0	1
Rob Harden	36	6-12	0-0	-	1	4	3	12
Tony Sommers	32	6-10	1-3	-	6	1	4	13
	MIN	FGM-A	FTM-A	OFF	REB	AST	PF	PTS
Quentin Stephens	20	0-1	0-4	-	3	0	2	0
Tony Ronzone	9	0-1	0-0	-	1	0	1	0
Curtis High	34	6-12	2-2	-	3	1	5	14
Mike Juby	1	0-0	0-0	-	0	0	0	0
TOTALS		FGM-A	FTM-A	OFF	REB	AST	PF	PTS
		25-55	6-13	-	27	6	19	56

NORTH CAROLINA STATE WOLFPACK

	MIN	FGM-A	FTM-A	OFF	REB	AST	PF	PTS
Russell Pierre	16	1-4	0-0	-	3	0	1	2
Terry Gannon	29	2-11	4-4	-	1	5	0	8
Lorenzo Charles	34	8-14	6-7	-	12	0	1	22

	MIN	FGM-A	FTM-A	OFF	REB	AST	PF	PTS
Spud Webb	39	4-8	3-4	-	0	4	3	11
Cozell McQueen	29	2-3	0-0	-	4	1	4	4
	MIN	FGM-A	FTM-A	OFF	REB	AST	PF	PTS
Bennie Bolton	11	3-4	0-0	-	5	0	1	6
Quentin Jackson	1	0-1	0-0	-	0	0	0	0
Nate Mcmillan	29	3-5	1-3	-	3	2	4	7
Ernie Myers	12	2-6	1-1	-	6	1	2	5
TOTALS		FGM-A	FTM-A	OFF	REB	AST	PF	PTS
		25-56	15-19	-	34	13	16	65

7. Alabama 50
10. Arizona 41

Many thought Lute Olson was nuts for leaving Iowa's successful program for one whose legacy was as barren as the desert surrounding its campus. But in only his second year in Tucson he led the Wildcats to just their fourth NCAA tournament appearance.

Olson knew that nerves might be an issue. "I expect them to be nervous," he said of his players. "But I don't expect them to be so nervous that it affects their performance."

Perhaps he didn't know his team as well as he thought. The young Wildcats seemed flustered by Alabama's aggressive defense and shot only 29 percent from the floor. "We played well enough to win defensively, but we couldn't hit our shots," Olson lamented. "Alabama played the best man-to-man defense that I've ever seen."

The Crimson Tide got a big late-season boost when Derrick McKey was put in the starting lineup, but the freshman laid an egg in his tournament debut, scoring zero points before fouling out. Reliable veterans Buck Johnson and Bobby Lee Hurt were able to pick up the slack, however, combining for 26 points. Bama, which never trailed, sank 12 straight free throws in the closing minutes to ice the victory and finish off the Pac-10, which went 0-4 in the 1985 tournament.

ALABAMA CRIMSON TIDE								
	MIN	FGM-A	FTM-A	OFF	REB	AST	PF	PTS
Darrell Neal	16	1-4	0-0	-	3	0	2	2
Terry Coner	38	2-7	6-6	-	4	5	2	10
Jim Farmer	23	4-7	0-0	-	4	0	0	8
Derrick McKey	27	0-2	0-0	-	3	2	5	0
Buck Johnson	36	5-6	2-4	-	5	2	4	12
	MIN	FGM-A	FTM-A	OFF	REB	AST	PF	PTS
Mark Gottfried	22	1-3	2-2	-	2	0	1	4
Bobby Lee Hurt	38	5-7	4-9	-	6	0	4	14

TOTALS	FGM-A	FTM-A	OFF	REB	AST	PF	PTS
	18-36	14-21	-	27	9	18	50

ARIZONA WILDCATS

	MIN	FGM-A	FTM-A	OFF	REB	AST	PF	PTS
Morgan Taylor	26	0-5	4-6	-	6	0	5	4
Peter Williams	40	3-11	4-5	-	7	1	4	10
Eddie Smith	38	2-11	5-6	-	6	2	4	9
Steve Kerr	40	4-8	0-0	-	5	0	0	8
Brock Brunkhorst	31	1-7	0-0	-	2	3	1	2
	MIN	FGM-A	FTM-A	OFF	REB	AST	PF	PTS
Craig McMillan	25	4-6	0-2	-	1	1	4	8
TOTALS		FGM-A	FTM-A	OFF	REB	AST	PF	PTS
		14-48	13-19	-	27	7	18	41

2. Virginia Commonwealth 81
15. Marshall 65

Was it an abuse of power or a well-deserved reward for a relatively unknown school? Some were shocked when Virginia Commonwealth received a No. 2 seed, but maybe it shouldn't have been a surprise considering Sun Belt Conference commissioner Vic Bubas also happened to be the head of the selection committee.

Marshall had its own share of doubters. The Thundering Herd, whose long journey to Albuquerque began with a caravan of Cadillacs to the airport, were considered a 50,000-1 shot to win it all, but coach Rick Huckabay wasn't fazed. "We've overcome huge odds in the past," he said.

What his team couldn't overcome were VCU senior guards Rolando Lamb and Calvin Douglas. They formed one of the best backcourts in the country and Marshall found out why as Lamb produced 30 points and 6 steals and Duncan added 19 points and 5 assists.

The Herd got off to a quick 6-2 lead as freshman Skip Henderson made three straight shots. But the experienced Rams, playing in their third straight NCAA tournament, settled down and proceeded to dominate Marshall behind a blistering offense that made 56 percent of its shots.

MARSHALL THUNDERING HERD

	MIN	FGM-A	FTM-A	OFF	REB	AST	PF	PTS
Jeff Battle	28	4-12	2-2	-	4	4	4	10
Kyle Taylor	7	1-4	0-0	-	1	1	1	2
John Amendola	2	0-2	0-0	-	1	0	0	0
Jeff Richardson	25	3-8	1-2	-	4	0	4	7

	MIN	FGM-A	FTM-A	OFF	REB	AST	PF	PTS
James Roberts	8	0-0	0-0	-	1	0	2	0
Martin Smith	2	0-0	0-0	-	0	0	0	0
Tom Curry	14	1-4	2-3	-	1	0	4	4
Maurice Bryson	2	0-1	1-2	-	2	0	1	1
Robert Eppes	15	4-5	2-2	-	3	0	1	10
Skip Henderson	33	8-15	3-4	-	4	3	3	19
Bruce Morris	10	0-2	0-0	-	1	0	0	0
Rodney Holden	17	3-3	0-2	-	6	0	2	6
Jeff Guthrie	37	2-6	2-2	-	5	1	4	6
TOTALS		FGM-A	FTM-A	OFF	REB	AST	PF	PTS
		26-62	13-19	-	33	9	26	65

VIRGINIA COMMONWEALTH RAMS

	MIN	FGM-A	FTM-A	OFF	REB	AST	PF	PTS
Bruce Allen	1	0-0	1-3	-	0	0	0	1
Neil Wake	15	2-3	3-4	-	3	1	4	7
Alvin Robinson	10	0-0	0-0	-	2	0	4	0
Mike Schlegel	38	5-10	4-7	-	6	3	3	14
Phil Stinnie	3	0-0	0-0	-	1	0	0	0
Robert Dickerson	20	1-3	0-0	-	3	0	2	2
Don Franco	2	0-0	2-2	-	2	0	0	2
Michael Brown	39	3-6	0-1	-	3	4	4	6
Rolando Lamb	36	12-17	6-7	-	4	4	3	30
Calvin Duncan	36	6-13	7-9	-	4	5	0	19
TOTALS		FGM-A	FTM-A	OFF	REB	AST	PF	PTS
		29-52	23-33	-	28	17	20	81

Southeast Region

March 14

South Bend, IN

11. Auburn 59

6. Purdue 58

Foul shooting wasn't Chris Morris' strong suit, but his coach wasn't concerned. The freshman, who made only 64 percent of his free throws during the season, stepped to the line with 14 seconds left and sank the shot that gave Auburn the one-point win.

"He's hit some big free throws for us," Tigers coach Sonny Smith said. "He started the year a very poor free throw shooter, but now we'd like to have him on the line as much as anybody."

Purdue still had a chance after Morris' heroics. But James Bullock's short jumper with 2 seconds left clanged off the rim and Auburn had its first-ever NCAA tournament victory.

The Boilermakers had to play catch-up the entire game. A late spurt, capped by freshman Troy Lewis' basket with 55 seconds remaining, tied the game, setting the stage for Morris' big moment. Chuck "The Rifleman" Person was the game's leading scorer with 20 points, his 66th straight game in double digits.

Auburn's win, plus the school's first SEC tournament championship the week before, appeared to be going-away presents for Smith, who had surprisingly announced his resignation Feb. 8. But Smith would drop another bombshell after the Tigers' tourney run when he said that he would be staying after all.

PURDUE BOILERMAKERS

	MIN	FGM-A	FTM-A	OFF	REB	AST	PF	PTS
Mark Atkinson	36	0-2	0-0	-	3	2	4	0
Steve Reid	39	9-17	0-2	-	3	6	4	18
Herbert Robinson	5	0-0	0-0	-	0	0	0	0
Todd Mitchell	11	0-2	0-0	-	2	0	2	0
Jim Bullock	40	6-15	1-3	-	10	0	4	13
	MIN	FGM-A	FTM-A	OFF	REB	AST	PF	PTS
Mack Gadis	10	0-1	0-0	-	0	0	0	0
Troy Lewis	30	9-17	1-2	-	2	1	1	19
Robert Littlejohn	29	3-5	2-2	-	9	0	0	8
TOTALS		FGM-A	FTM-A	OFF	REB	AST	PF	PTS
		27-59	4-9	-	29	9	15	58

AUBURN TIGERS

	MIN	FGM-A	FTM-A	OFF	REB	AST	PF	PTS
Chuck Person	39	9-17	2-2	-	8	0	3	20
Gerald White	37	3-5	1-4	-	5	4	1	7
Frank Ford	39	4-7	1-1	-	6	3	2	9
Carey Holland	10	1-1	0-0	-	0	0	1	2
Johnny Lynn	7	0-2	0-0	-	1	0	0	0
	MIN	FGM-A	FTM-A	OFF	REB	AST	PF	PTS
Darren Guest	3	0-1	0-0	-	0	0	0	0
Jeff Moore	28	1-5	0-0	-	7	1	3	2
Chris Morris	37	9-14	1-2	-	3	0	1	19
TOTALS		FGM-A	FTM-A	OFF	REB	AST	PF	PTS
		27-52	5-9	-	30	8	11	59

3. Kansas 49
14. Ohio 38

For one half, at least, Ohio's stall was as mighty as Kansas' high-powered offense. The out-manned Bobcats brought the "action" to a near standstill in the opening 20 minutes and returned to the locker room trailing only 18-15.

Kansas, which averaged 76 points a game for the season, kept its composure, and eventually the Jayhawks' superior talent took over. Calvin Thompson scored 11 of his team-high 12 points in the second half as 13th-ranked Kansas let loose its running attack and pulled away, despite finishing with its second-lowest point total on the season and a meager 28 shot attempts.

In his first exposure to the NCAA tournament, freshman sensation and future Final Four Most Outstanding Player Danny Manning had 9 points and 6 rebounds.

Unfortunately for Ohio, it could not take advantage of its limited opportunities. Kansas' zone defenses held the Bobcats to just 33 percent shooting. But Nebraska officials apparently were able to stay awake long enough to gain an appreciation for coach Danny Nee, who would be hired by the Cornhuskers the following year.

OHIO BOBCATS								
	MIN	FGM-A	FTM-A	OFF	REB	AST	PF	PTS
Paul Baron	34	1-3	2-5	-	6	2	4	4
Robert Tatum	37	1-8	0-0	-	0	2	5	2
Vic Alexander	32	6-9	3-3	-	3	0	3	15
Eddie Washington	3	0-3	0-0	-	0	0	1	0
John Rhodes	2	0-0	0-0	-	3	0	2	0
	MIN	FGM-A	FTM-A	OFF	REB	AST	PF	PTS
Rick Scarberry	27	2-7	0-0	-	1	1	1	4
Henry Smith	17	2-7	0-1	-	5	0	1	4
Roger Smith	2	0-0	2-2	-	1	0	0	2
Rich Stanfel	6	0-0	0-0	-	0	0	0	0
Eddie Hicks	37	0-3	3-4	-	7	0	3	3
Jamie Brock	1	1-1	0-0	-	0	0	1	2
Marty Lehmann	2	1-1	0-0	-	0	0	1	2
TOTALS		FGM-A	FTM-A	OFF	REB	AST	PF	PTS
		14-42	10-15	-	26	5	22	38

KANSAS JAYHAWKS								
	MIN	FGM-A	FTM-A	OFF	REB	AST	PF	PTS

	MIN	FGM-A	FTM-A		OFF	REB	AST	PF	PTS
Mark Pellock	1	0-0	0-1	-	0	0	0		0
Chris Piper	2	0-0	0-0	-	0	0	0		0
Altonio Campbell	2	0-0	0-2	-	0	0	1		0
Calvin Thompson	34	3-7	6-8	-	2	1	4		12
Milt Newton	6	0-0	1-2	-	1	0	0		1

	MIN	FGM-A	FTM-A	OFF	REB	AST	PF	PTS
Mark Turgeon	2	0-0	0-0	-	0	2	1	0
Thomas Boyle	1	0-0	3-4	-	0	0	0	3
Danny Manning	38	4-5	1-2	-	6	1	4	9
Ronald Kellogg	38	4-9	2-3	-	1	0	3	10
Jeff Johnson	1	0-0	0-0	-	0	0	0	0
Greg Dreiling	36	3-4	4-4	-	8	0	3	10
Cedric Hunter	37	2-3	0-2	-	3	4	1	4
Rodney Hull	2	0-0	0-0	-	0	0	0	0
TOTALS		FGM-A	FTM-A	OFF	REB	AST	PF	PTS
		16-28	17-28	-	21	8	17	49

7. Notre Dame 79
10. Oregon State 70

As if playing on his home court wasn't advantage enough, Fighting Irish coach Digger Phelps got some words of advice on Oregon State from an old friend. Phelps said he consulted with California head coach Dick Kuchen, who was once Phelps' top assistant and whose Bears faced the Beavers three times in 1984-85, for tips on his first-round foe.

"We talked last night," Phelps said. "I think I mentioned if he happened to know anything about Oregon State."

Beavers assistant coach Lanny Van Eman didn't see this as just a cordial chat. "Ethics are involved here," Van Eman fumed. "That's probably been violated a little bit, but we wouldn't violate that."

If Kuchen offered tips on how to attack Oregon State's defense, they certainly seemed to work. Notre Dame, playing its first NCAA tournament game since BYU's Danny Ainge broke its heart in 1981, shot 64 percent from its familiar home floor. Freshman David Rivers was a blur in racking up 21 points as the Irish, who never trailed, amassed a 13-point second-half lead. But Oregon State rallied to tie the game at 56 behind A.C. Green, the Pac-10's top scorer and rebounder, whose final college game included 26 points and 12 boards.

Rivers went on an 8-point scoring binge to rebuild the Irish lead, and then deft shooting from the foul line settled the game. Rivers, Tim Kempton and Scott Hicks made six straight from the stripe in the final minute for Notre Dame, which sank 19 of 21 on the night. "I did take control in the last seven minutes," Rivers said matter-of-factly. "That's my job."

OREGON STATE BEAVERS

	MIN	FGM-A	FTM-A	OFF	REB	AST	PF	PTS
Steve Woodside	39	2-8	1-2	-	4	0	2	5
Darryl Flowers	37	6-12	1-1	-	1	3	4	13
Mark Kaska	3	0-0	0-0	-	0	0	1	0
Eric Knox	19	2-5	0-0	-	1	0	3	4
Pat Giusti	1	0-0	0-0	-	0	0	0	0
	MIN	FGM-A	FTM-A	OFF	REB	AST	PF	PTS
Darrin Houston	26	6-13	0-1	-	1	0	1	12
Dean Derrah	4	0-0	0-0	-	0	0	1	0
Tyrone Miller	31	3-4	4-4	-	3	1	5	10
A.C. Green	40	10-14	6-9	-	12	1	1	26
TOTALS		FGM-A	FTM-A	OFF	REB	AST	PF	PTS
		29-56	12-17	-	22	5	18	70

NOTRE DAME FIGHTING IRISH

	MIN	FGM-A	FTM-A	OFF	REB	AST	PF	PTS
Ken Barlow	15	0-3	0-0	-	1	1	2	0
Joseph Price	34	7-9	2-2	-	3	2	4	16
David Rivers	36	8-12	5-6	-	1	3	1	21
Gary Voce	1	0-0	0-0	-	0	0	0	0
Scott Hicks	35	5-8	4-4	-	5	0	2	14
	MIN	FGM-A	FTM-A	OFF	REB	AST	PF	PTS
Donald Royal	29	4-7	4-4	-	4	0	5	12
Tim Kempton	27	3-5	3-4	-	5	0	3	9
Jim Dolan	19	3-3	1-1	-	6	0	2	7
Dan Duff	4	0-0	0-0	-	1	0	0	0
TOTALS		FGM-A	FTM-A	OFF	REB	AST	PF	PTS
		30-47	19-21	-	26	6	19	79

2. North Carolina 76
15. Middle Tennessee State 57

Were these the Blue Raiders or the Blue Devils?

North Carolina might have been wondering if archrival Duke had slipped on the Middle Tennessee State uniforms prior to tip-off, considering how tough the fifth-place finisher in the Ohio Valley Conference proved to be for three quarters of the game. Kim Cooksey's 10 first-half points helped the Raiders take an early seven-point lead, and they still held a one-point advantage with 11:23 left in the game.

Then Brad Daugherty took over. The 7-foot junior scored four quick baskets as part of his 14-point second half, propelling the seventh-ranked Tar Heels on a 28-8 run and a comfortable victory. "We wanted to calm down, take our time and use our size to our advantage," said Daugherty, who finished with 25 points and 11 rebounds. Fellow front-courter Joe Wolf also had a double-double (18 points, 11 boards).

Victory did not come cheaply, however. Starting guard Steve Hale was lost for the rest of the tournament when a hard foul late in the game sent him crashing to the floor, causing a separated shoulder.

MIDDLE TENNESSEE STATE BLUE RAIDERS

	MIN	FGM-A	FTM-A	OFF	REB	AST	PF	PTS
Kerry Hammonds	40	3-18	3-4	-	7	0	4	9
Lonnie Thompson	37	10-17	0-0	-	8	3	4	20
Kim Cooksey	38	7-22	0-1	-	5	2	3	14
Russell Smith	16	0-2	0-0	-	1	0	2	0
James Johnson	26	4-6	0-2	-	6	0	5	8
	MIN	FGM-A	FTM-A	OFF	REB	AST	PF	PTS
Billy Miller	24	1-2	0-0	-	2	0	3	2
Greg Stevenson	5	2-3	0-0	-	1	1	0	4
Neal Murray	14	0-0	0-0	-	1	1	0	0
TOTALS		FGM-A	FTM-A	OFF	REB	AST	PF	PTS
		27-70	3-7	-	31	7	21	57

NORTH CAROLINA TAR HEELS

	MIN	FGM-A	FTM-A	OFF	REB	AST	PF	PTS
Buzz Peterson	18	1-2	4-4	-	2	1	0	6
Dave Popson	9	1-4	0-0	-	1	0	1	2
Steve Hale	32	1-4	0-0	-	4	2	1	2
Brad Daugherty	35	11-15	3-4	-	11	1	3	25
Joe Wolf	34	6-9	6-7	-	11	0	2	18
	MIN	FGM-A	FTM-A	OFF	REB	AST	PF	PTS
Kenny Smith	39	1-6	4-4	-	4	7	1	6
Ranzino Smith	3	0-1	0-0	-	1	0	0	0
Warren Martin	23	6-8	2-5	-	7	0	4	14
Curtis Hunter	7	1-4	1-3	-	0	0	0	3

TOTALS	FGM-A	FTM-A	OFF	REB	AST	PF	PTS
	28-53	20-27	-	41	11	12	76

March 15
Dayton, OH
1. Michigan 59
16. Fairleigh Dickinson 55

The new 64-team NCAA tournament setup meant many Rodney Dangerfield teams would be hunting for a little respect. In the case of Fairleigh Dickinson, it almost got so much more.

"We just said, 'Who's Fairleigh Dickinson?'", freshman Gary Grant recalled of Michigan's reaction when it learned its opening-round opponent. "I never heard of them," Big Ten player of the year Roy Tarpley added. Dick Vitale blasted the inclusion of small-conference teams in the expanded tournament, singling out FDU as one supposed lightweight that would get trounced. Knights coach Tom Green got in on the act, saying that he would "get about four transfers in a hurry" when asked how he would prepare for the Big Ten champs.

The second-ranked Wolverines, in the NCAA tournament for the first time in eight years, thoroughly dominated the Big Ten, closing the season with 16 straight wins and clinching the conference championship with three weeks left in the season. Fairleigh Dickinson of little Teaneck, N.J., meanwhile, was making its first-ever postseason appearance.

"I'll tell you this, we're not going to overlook them," Michigan coach Bill Frieder assured. His players didn't seem to get the message. FDU used a deliberate pace on offense to fluster the high-tempo Wolverines and control the action for most of the game. The Knights held a 32-22 lead with 14:22 remaining, no doubt sparking a flurry of "you've got to turn on your TV" phone calls throughout the country. "They looked like they were ready to give up," FDU's Larry Hampton said. "I thought we had them then."

With backcourt stars Grant and Antoine Joubert (combined 4-of-17 shooting and 9 points) muddling through off days and Tarpley saddled with four fouls, the Wolverines were rescued by backups Leslie Rockymore and Robert Henderson. Rockymore struck for five straight points to give Michigan a 46-41 lead, while Henderson dominated on the defensive end with three key steals. Michigan used a 25-7 spurt to build a seemingly safe 55-43 advantage, but the pesky Knights were not through, even with three key players fouled out.

FDU roared back, scoring with 10 seconds left to cut the deficit to two. But Tarpley (15 points, 13 rebounds) sank two free throws for the final margin of victory. "As far as I'm concerned, we should have a shot clock," a frazzled Frieder said afterwards. "I hope we play a little harder, a little smarter and a little more under control next time."

A proud Green spoke out for the little guy in the brave new world of the 64-team field: "I think we belong in the tournament no matter what anyone else says. We didn't think it was impossible to beat Michigan. You might have."

MICHIGAN WOLVERINES

	MIN	FGM-A	FTM-A	OFF	REB	AST	PF	PTS
Roy Tarpley	31	6-14	3-4	-	13	0	4	15
Garde Thompson	12	0-2	2-2	-	2	0	3	2
Richard Rellford	25	4-8	2-2	-	4	2	2	10
Butch Wade	26	1-2	1-3	-	5	0	4	3
Leslie Rockymore	19	3-6	4-7	-	1	3	1	10
	MIN	FGM-A	FTM-A	OFF	REB	AST	PF	PTS
Stephen Stoyko	1	0-0	0-0	-	0	0	0	0
Antoine Joubert	27	1-9	1-1	-	3	5	4	3
Robert Henderson	25	4-5	2-3	-	4	1	1	10
Gary Grant	34	3-8	0-0	-	3	6	2	6
TOTALS		FGM-A	FTM-A	OFF	REB	AST	PF	PTS
		22-54	15-22	-	35	17	21	59

FAIRLEIGH DICKINSON KNIGHTS

	MIN	FGM-A	FTM-A	OFF	REB	AST	PF	PTS
Steve Malloy	3	0-0	0-0	-	1	0	0	0
Lonnie Jackson	30	3-3	2-3	-	1	4	3	8
Rob Duncan	15	1-4	3-3	-	3	0	2	5
Damari Riddick	24	3-5	0-2	-	1	1	5	6
Lance Thomas	2	0-1	0-0	-	0	0	0	0
	MIN	FGM-A	FTM-A	OFF	REB	AST	PF	PTS
Larry Hampton	35	4-9	2-4	-	6	1	5	10
Fred Collins	38	2-6	2-4	-	3	4	5	6
Gary Wilson	34	2-2	8-8	-	5	0	5	12
Akila Shokai	1	0-0	0-0	-	0	0	0	0
Jaime Latney	18	4-8	0-0	-	5	1	1	8
TOTALS		FGM-A	FTM-A	OFF	REB	AST	PF	PTS
		19-38	17-24	-	25	11	26	55

8. Villanova 51
9. Dayton 49

One of the greatest Cinderellas of all time was treated rather rudely by the selection committee before its journey even began. Villanova, 19-10 on the season and third in the Big East, had to face a pesky Dayton team on the Flyers' own turf, where they had lost only twice all year.

"That's just one of those things," diplomatic Wildcats coach Rollie Massimino said. "At this stage of the game, you've just got to be happy to be in it."

Working in 'Nova's favor was the fact that it had won its seven previous opening NCAA tournament games. Another plus for the Cats was Ed Pinckney. The senior center was the best player on the floor, finishing with a game-high 20 points while completely dominating Dayton star Dave Colbert, whose 5 points were 13 below his season average.

"We're just too small," Flyers coach Don Donoher bemoaned. "And Pinckney is such a force in there, it was hard for Dave to go inside to get post-up shots."

Still, Dayton was able to go toe-to-toe with Villanova thanks to some dead-eye foul shooting. The Flyers made all 17 of their attempts and had the sellout crowd of 13,260 roaring when they took a 49-47 lead, but Pinckney silenced the throng with a game-tying layup with 3:34 remaining. Then Harold Pressley administered what Donoher called "the back-breaker" when he stole the ball with three minutes to go, setting the stage for Harold Jensen's go-ahead layup with 1:10 on the clock.

"I didn't see anybody in the middle. So I saw a chance. I said what the hell," Jensen said of his heroic shot.

Dayton came oh-so-close to forcing overtime, but Sedric Toney's put-back with three seconds left rimmed out. "It did everything but go in," Donoher said. "It rolled around a couple times and then came out." Thanks to that, the clock did not strike midnight early for destiny's Cats.

DAYTON FLYERS								
	MIN	FGM-A	FTM-A	OFF	REB	AST	PF	PTS
Jeff Zern	17	1-2	0-0	-	1	0	5	2
Dan Christie	7	0-1	0-0	-	1	1	1	0
Dave Colbert	39	2-5	1-1	-	6	1	3	5
Sedric Toney	37	5-16	2-2	-	0	4	0	12
Larry Schellenberg	40	3-6	6-6	-	5	4	2	12
	MIN	FGM-A	FTM-A	OFF	REB	AST	PF	PTS
Ted Harris	1	0-0	0-0	-	0	0	0	0
Damon Goodwin	38	4-8	8-8	-	9	2	3	16
Anthony Grant	21	1-5	0-0	-	8	0	2	2
TOTALS		FGM-A	FTM-A	OFF	REB	AST	PF	PTS

| | | 16-43 | 17-17 | - | 30 | 12 | 16 | 49 |

VILLANOVA WILDCATS								
	MIN	FGM-A	FTM-A	OFF	REB	AST	PF	PTS
Ed Pinckney	40	6-10	8-13	-	6	1	3	20
Mark Plansky	1	0-0	0-0	-	1	0	1	0
Harold Pressley	38	4-9	0-1	-	5	1	3	8
Dwight Wilbur	23	1-5	0-0	-	1	1	2	2
Dwayne McClain	36	5-9	1-1	-	5	3	4	11
	MIN	FGM-A	FTM-A	OFF	REB	AST	PF	PTS
Chuck Everson	1	0-0	0-0	-	0	0	0	0
Harold Jensen	24	3-5	2-2	-	0	1	1	8
Gary McLain	37	1-4	0-0	-	2	1	3	2
TOTALS		FGM-A	FTM-A	OFF	REB	AST	PF	PTS
		20-42	11-17	-	20	8	17	51

5. Maryland 69
12. Miami (OH) 68 (OT)

All it took was a well-timed shove to push Maryland into the second round after 45 harrowing minutes and a near-upset from a little-known team led by a future NBA star.

The Redskins clung to a one-point lead with 17 seconds left in overtime when Ron Harper, who would win five NBA title after being a draft lottery pick in 1986, tried to inbound the ball to Todd Staker. But Maryland's Adrian Branch knocked Staker out of the way, allowing Branch to grab the loose ball and put up a shot. It missed, but teammate Jeff Adkins was in the right place at the right time as he rebounded and laid in the winning basket.

"The guy (Harper) was having a hard time finding his receiver," Branch said of the controversial play. "I kind of gave the guy a push and he lost the ball. I was waiting for the whistle."

Maryland superstar Len Bias helped offset Harper's game-high 26 points with 25 of his own before fouling out late in overtime, long after the Terrapins had wasted a 9-point lead with less than 12 minutes left thanks largely to an ill-timed stall tactic by coach Lefty Driesell, whose team was not used to playing without a shot clock.

"I definitely think we held the ball too soon," Driesell said. With his team down late in overtime, Driesell sensed doom: "I said, 'Hey, the Lord don't want me to win today. I figured we'd get outta here and go home." Instead, he got a friendly nudge and a new life.

MARYLAND TERRAPINS

	MIN	FGM-A	FTM-A	OFF	REB	AST	PF	PTS
Len Bias	42	10-17	5-6	-	9	1	5	25
Adrian Branch	45	9-20	6-6	-	5	0	3	24
Derrick Lewis	25	1-1	0-0	-	6	1	5	2
Keith Gatlin	44	1-6	0-0	-	3	10	2	2
Jeff Adkins	45	6-9	0-0	-	2	3	2	12
	MIN	FGM-A	FTM-A	OFF	REB	AST	PF	PTS
Terry Long	7	0-0	0-0	-	0	0	1	0
Thomas Jones	15	2-2	0-0	-	0	0	1	4
Jeff Baxter	2	0-0	0-0	-	0	0	0	0
TOTALS		FGM-A	FTM-A	OFF	REB	AST	PF	PTS
		29-55	11-12	-	25	15	19	69

MIAMI (OHIO) REDSKINS

	MIN	FGM-A	FTM-A	OFF	REB	AST	PF	PTS
Ron Harper	44	9-14	8-11	-	8	3	4	26
Ron Hunter	22	3-9	1-2	-	3	0	2	7
Tim Lampe	18	1-4	0-0	-	2	0	0	2
Eddie Schilling	30	2-6	0-0	-	4	6	2	4
Eric Newsome	41	4-10	7-9	-	2	2	3	15
	MIN	FGM-A	FTM-A	OFF	REB	AST	PF	PTS
Mike Hall	12	0-2	0-0	-	2	0	1	0
Todd Staker	32	3-8	0-0	-	3	1	2	6
Lamont Hanna	26	4-6	0-0	-	8	0	1	8
TOTALS		FGM-A	FTM-A	OFF	REB	AST	PF	PTS
		26-59	16-22	-	32	12	14	68

13. Navy 78
4. LSU 55

LSU was sailing smoothly after winning the SEC tournament, only to be sunk by a Navy that few thought had much of a chance. David "The Admiral" Robinson had a national coming-out party with 18 points and 18 rebounds and the Midshipmen made the most of a continuous parade to the foul line, where they made 34 of their 43 attempts.

The Tigers' upset loss was surprising enough, but the ease with which the Middies won was what had people talking afterwards.

"I didn't think we could blow out anybody," Navy coach Paul Evans said. "But I thought we could play with anybody." Evans' counterpart, Dale Brown, cited "mental burnout" as the explanation for the shocking outcome. "It wasn't a fluke. The points are almost incredible," a shell-shocked Brown said. "They totally dominated us. You have moments of embarrassment. That's what it is."

Nikita Wilson, LSU's leading scorer, was held to 9 points before fouling out with more than eight minutes left as nothing went right for the Tigers. They made only 34 percent of their shots and committed 16 more fouls than their disciplined foe. Navy, which led 28-24 at halftime, pulled away in the final 20 minutes behind the game's top scorer, Vernon Butler, who finished with 20 points and made all 10 free throws.

LOUISIANA STATE TIGERS								
	MIN	FGM-A	FTM-A	OFF	REB	AST	PF	PTS
John Williams	-	6-8	0-0	-	5	1	4	12
Jerry Reynolds	-	1-8	2-2	-	4	2	3	4
Nikita Wilson	-	4-8	1-2	-	5	0	5	9
Derrick Taylor	-	2-13	0-0	-	1	3	4	4
Don Redden	-	1-5	0-0	-	3	2	2	2
	MIN	FGM-A	FTM-A	OFF	REB	AST	PF	PTS
Ricky Blanton	-	1-1	2-4	-	3	1	3	4
Dennis Brown	-	4-10	0-0	-	2	2	3	8
Oliver Brown	-	1-3	2-2	-	5	1	2	4
Jose Vargas	-	1-2	0-0	-	0	0	3	2
Zoran Jovanovich	-	0-1	0-0	-	2	0	1	0
Anthony Wilson	-	1-6	0-0	-	1	0	1	2
Ocie Conley	-	1-3	2-3	-	2	0	0	4
Neboisha Bukumirovich	-	0-0	0-0	-	0	2	1	0
TOTALS		FGM-A	FTM-A	OFF	REB	AST	PF	PTS
		23-68	9-13	-	33	14	32	55

NAVY MIDSHIPMEN								
	MIN	FGM-A	FTM-A	OFF	REB	AST	PF	PTS
Vernon Butler	37	5-11	10-10	-	9	2	4	20
Kylor Whitaker	38	2-7	9-10	-	4	2	2	13
David Robinson	38	8-14	2-7	-	18	0	2	18
Cliff Rees	27	1-3	2-2	-	1	2	1	4
Doug Wojcik	36	5-7	8-8	-	3	8	2	18
	MIN	FGM-A	FTM-A	OFF	REB	AST	PF	PTS
Carl Liebert	7	0-1	0-2	-	1	0	1	0
Tony Wells	7	0-1	0-0	-	1	0	2	0

Kevin Coyne	2	0-0	1-2	-	0	0	0	1
Sly Mata	2	0-0	2-2	-	0	0	0	2
Carey Manhertz	2	0-0	0-0	-	1	0	2	0
Mike Klooster	2	0-0	0-0	-	0	0	0	0
James Reed	1	0-0	0-0	-	0	0	0	0
Mike Kurka	1	1-1	0-0	-	0	0	0	2
TOTALS		FGM-A	FTM-A	OFF	REB	AST	PF	PTS
		22-45	34-43	-	38	14	16	78

Midwest Region

March 14
Tulsa, OK
1. Oklahoma 96
16. North Carolina A&T 83

It was a classic David vs. Goliath matchup. Fourth-ranked Big Eight champion Oklahoma against a Mid-Eastern Athletic Conference team that had losses to the likes of Delaware State and Appalachian State. 6-foot-9 All-American scoring machine Wayman Tisdale against a squad with no one taller than 6-6.

In the end, the game would go largely according to script, but the spunky Aggies from the Tar Heel State, who were in the midst of a streak of seven straight NCAA tournament appearances, did their small-conference brethren proud. Tisdale dominated, as expected, with 28 points, 12 rebounds and four old-fashioned 3-point plays.

Nevertheless, A&T found itself down only 6 points with just under 12 minutes left, thanks in part to a 10-0 run to start the second half. But the Sooners snapped out of their funk with an 11-2 spurt of their own to salt the game away.

With his pesky but overmatched team eliminated, Aggies coach Don Corbett was naturally asked about a possible national championship showdown between heavyweights Oklahoma and Georgetown and a head-to-head duel of perhaps the two best players in the country – Tisdale and the Hoyas' Patrick Ewing. Corbett's team had faced both the Hoyas (five-point loss in December) and Sooners that season.

"The press would hurt them (the Sooners). They don't handle it well," Corbett said. "Georgetown presses you for 40 minutes. Tisdale had things his own way with us, but down inside with Ewing it would be a different matter."

OKLAHOMA SOONERS								
	MIN	FGM-A	FTM-A	OFF	REB	AST	PF	PTS
Anthony Bowie	34	5-12	3-3	2	7	6	2	13
Darryl Kennedy	33	8-15	1-1	4	10	1	4	17

	MIN	FGM-A	FTM-A	OFF	REB	AST	PF	PTS
Wayman Tisdale	38	12-16	4-4	5	12	0	3	28
Tim McCalister	38	9-17	5-6	1	1	5	1	23
Linwood Davis	22	0-3	0-0	0	1	8	0	0
	MIN	FGM-A	FTM-A	OFF	REB	AST	PF	PTS
Shawn Clark	26	3-7	4-4	1	3	3	1	10
David Johnson	9	2-4	1-2	1	1	1	2	5
TOTALS		FGM-A	FTM-A	OFF	REB	AST	PF	PTS
		39-74	18-20	14	35	24	13	96

NORTH CAROLINA A&T AGGIES

	MIN	FGM-A	FTM-A	OFF	REB	AST	PF	PTS
Jimmy Brown	39	8-17	4-8	4	8	2	4	20
George Cale	38	10-14	0-0	3	5	2	3	20
Claude Williams	25	3-9	2-4	3	8	3	5	8
Thomas Griffis	36	4-5	0-0	1	4	4	1	8
Eric Boyd	38	6-15	6-6	0	2	2	3	18
	MIN	FGM-A	FTM-A	OFF	REB	AST	PF	PTS
Mitch Braswell	15	3-7	1-2	1	3	0	3	7
Lee Robinson	8	1-2	0-0	0	0	0	0	2
Mark Gaither	1	0-1	0-0	0	0	0	0	0
TOTALS		FGM-A	FTM-A	OFF	REB	AST	PF	PTS
		35-70	13-20	12	30	13	19	83

9. Illinois State 58
8. Southern California 55

It usually isn't pretty, but taking care of the fundamentals often leads to victory. That lesson was repeated in Illinois State's hard-fought win that came about largely because of the Redbirds' excellence from the foul line late in the game.

Senior guard Michael McKenny guaranteed himself one more game by calmly sinking six free throws in one-and-one situations in the final two minutes to help Illinois State grind out a less-than-artistic victory.

"Hitting free throws down the stretch was paramount," Redbirds coach Bob Donewald said. "Some nights we're awful. We had the ball in the right hands of the right kids tonight." USC coach Stan Morrison echoed his counterpart. "The game was oftentimes like one you might play in your backyard. They shot free throws brilliantly."

Neither team ever led by more than nine points. The Trojans seemed to be in good shape with a seven-point edge early in the second half, but then the Redbirds clawed back and took the lead for good with 11:39 remaining.

SOUTHERN CALIFORNIA TROJANS

	MIN	FGM-A	FTM-A	OFF	REB	AST	PF	PTS
Derrick Dowell	30	2-7	0-0	1	3	3	1	4
Wayne Carlander	39	2-8	6-6	2	8	1	3	10
Clayton Olivier	28	2-5	3-4	1	5	0	2	7
Larry Friend	37	1-5	2-2	0	1	4	3	4
Ron Holmes	26	4-6	2-2	1	3	1	3	10
	MIN	FGM-A	FTM-A	OFF	REB	AST	PF	PTS
Glenn Smith	30	7-15	1-1	1	1	0	3	15
Charlie Simpson	10	2-3	1-2	0	0	0	4	5
TOTALS		FGM-A	FTM-A	OFF	REB	AST	PF	PTS
		20-49	15-17	6	21	9	19	55

ILLINOIS STATE REDBIRDS

	MIN	FGM-A	FTM-A	OFF	REB	AST	PF	PTS
Derrick Sanders	17	3-6	0-0	1	2	1	4	6
Lou Stefanovic	35	7-13	1-2	1	4	1	1	15
Bill Braksick	40	2-4	7-9	2	4	1	3	11
Michael McKenny	40	2-7	6-6	1	5	8	1	10
Rickie Johnson	36	4-8	4-6	1	10	1	3	12
	MIN	FGM-A	FTM-A	OFF	REB	AST	PF	PTS
Brad Duncan	20	2-3	0-0	1	2	1	1	4
Matt Taphorn	2	0-0	0-0	0	0	0	0	0
Tony Holifield	10	0-0	0-0	0	0	0	2	0
TOTALS		FGM-A	FTM-A	OFF	REB	AST	PF	PTS
		20-41	18-23	7	27	13	15	58

5. Louisiana Tech 78
12. Pittsburgh 54

For once "The Mailman" failed to deliver, but no one in Cajun Country was complaining. Robert Godbolt led a balanced Louisiana Tech attack with 18 points and Willie Bland chipped in 17 to offset the meager 9 points scored by superstar Karl Malone (7.5 below his season average) as the eighth-ranked Bulldogs ran their record to 28-2 with a cakewalk over the Big East's Panthers.

Tech was firing right from the start, scoring the game's first five points, and the Bulldogs amassed a 37-20 halftime lead that they built on in the second half. Pitt's cold shooting – 22 of 62 from the field for 35 percent – killed any hope for a rally, as did their whopping rebounding disadvantage (24 to the Bulldogs' 51). Tech's lead would grow as large as 35 points thanks to a stretch of 14 consecutive points.

While this tournament would be destined to go down as something of a coming-out party for the young Big East Conference, the fans from Louisiana were not impressed. They took to chanting "Big East, Big Deal" as they enjoyed the Bulldogs' romp.

Tech coach Andy Russo joined the chorus, saying, "I'm getting tired of hearing that the Southland Conference is inferior to some other conferences. Please tell everybody … to come on down to our conference and we'll take our chances."

LOUISIANA TECH BULLDOGS

	MIN	FGM-A	FTM-A	OFF	REB	AST	PF	PTS
Willie Simmons	27	5-10	3-6	5	10	0	4	13
Robert Godbolt	26	4-6	9-10	5	8	0	0	17
Karl Malone	25	4-10	1-2	6	10	2	3	9
Alan Davis	31	1-5	2-2	1	4	5	3	4
Wayne Smith	26	2-8	0-0	0	6	7	0	4
	MIN	FGM-A	FTM-A	OFF	REB	AST	PF	PTS
Willie Bland	21	7-10	2-4	4	4	1	2	16
Keith Troutman	4	0-0	0-0	0	0	0	1	0
Darryl Emerson	7	1-1	0-0	0	1	0	0	2
Roderick Hannibal	5	0-4	0-0	2	3	1	0	0
Kelvin Lewis	5	0-1	0-0	0	1	0	1	0
Adam Frank	14	4-5	3-4	0	3	1	0	11
David Jordan	9	1-3	0-0	1	1	0	2	2
TOTALS		FGM-A	FTM-A	OFF	REB	AST	PF	PTS
		29-63	20-28	24	51	17	16	78

PITTSBURGH PANTHERS

	MIN	FGM-A	FTM-A	OFF	REB	AST	PF	PTS
Daryl Shepherd	32	9-18	0-0	2	7	1	2	18
Andre Williams	8	0-1	0-0	1	2	0	5	0
Charles Smith	35	3-8	3-5	0	2	1	2	9
Joey David	18	2-4	0-0	0	1	0	0	4
Demetrius Gore	30	4-12	0-0	1	2	0	3	8
	MIN	FGM-A	FTM-A	OFF	REB	AST	PF	PTS
Curtis Aiken	15	0-1	0-2	0	2	3	1	0

		FGM-A	FTM-A	OFF	REB	AST	PF	PTS
Marlon Ferguson	7	2-3	2-2	2	3	0	0	6
John Blanton	1	0-0	0-0	0	0	1	0	0
Chas Thompson	9	0-2	0-0	0	0	3	2	0
Junie Lewis	8	1-3	4-4	0	0	1	1	6
Chip Watkins	8	1-3	0-0	0	0	0	3	2
Matt Miklasevich	14	0-4	0-0	1	2	1	1	0
Keith Armstrong	15	0-3	1-2	3	3	1	1	1
TOTALS		FGM-A	FTM-A	OFF	REB	AST	PF	PTS
		22-62	10-15	10	24	12	21	54

4. Ohio State 75
13. Iowa State 64

A man very familiar with Ohio State led Iowa State into battle with the Buckeyes in the Cyclones' first NCAA tournament in 41 years. Johnny Orr, who coached Michigan for 12 years before taking over the moribund Iowa State program in 1980, rebuilt the team with players plucked from Big Ten country, including future NBA players Jeff Hornacek (from Illinois) and Jeff Grayer (from Michigan).

"I don't think the kids get as big a kick out of playing Big Ten teams as I do," Orr said before the game. "It means more to me because we recruit those areas."

Orr would get an early start on his recruiting thanks to a pair of Buckeyes. Ronnie Stokes keyed a 10-2 run early in the half with a 3-point play after Dennis Hopson had helped Ohio State carve out a narrow halftime lead by firing in 15 of his 19 points in the opening 20 minutes. Barry Stevens, a two-time All-Big 8 pick, led the Cyclones with 24 points. Hornacek, meanwhile, gave little indication of the pro stardom that was to come, scoring only 5 points on 2-of-9 shooting.

Buckeyes coach Eldon Miller cited halftime defensive adjustments as the key after an explosive 39-37 first half. "I told them at the half it was going to get down to defense," Miller said. Keeping 7-foot center Brad Sellers in the paint paid dividends, as he swatted away four Iowa State shots after intermission, helping the limit the Cyclones to 27 second-half points.

OHIO STATE BUCKEYES								
	MIN	FGM-A	FTM-A	OFF	REB	AST	PF	PTS
Dennis Hopson	34	7-9	5-6	-	9	0	1	19
Joe Concheck	20	0-1	0-0	-	2	2	3	0
Brad Sellers	36	5-13	4-5	-	10	0	2	14
Ronnie Stokes	39	7-10	7-7	-	1	2	4	21
Troy Taylor	39	8-12	1-6	-	3	5	2	17
	MIN	FGM-A	FTM-A	OFF	REB	AST	PF	PTS
David Jones	30	2-5	0-0	-	2	3	4	4

	MIN	FGM-A	FTM-A	OFF	REB	AST	PF	PTS
Jim Honingford	1	0-0	0-0	-	0	0	0	0
Scott Anderson	1	0-0	0-0	-	0	0	0	0
TOTALS		FGM-A	FTM-A	OFF	REB	AST	PF	PTS
		29-50	17-24	-	27	12	16	75

IOWA STATE CYCLONES

	MIN	FGM-A	FTM-A	OFF	REB	AST	PF	PTS
Tom Peterson	28	1-1	0-0	-	1	1	2	2
Jeff Grayer	39	8-14	5-6	-	9	3	3	21
Sam Hill	22	2-4	0-0	-	5	0	2	4
Barry Stevens	38	12-24	0-1	-	4	2	2	24
Jeff Hornacek	38	2-9	1-2	-	3	7	4	5
	MIN	FGM-A	FTM-A	OFF	REB	AST	PF	PTS
Gary Thompkins	16	2-3	0-2	-	0	1	3	4
Lafester Rhodes	1	1-1	0-0	-	0	0	1	2
Ron Virgil	3	0-1	0-0	-	1	0	1	0
Eli Parker	1	1-1	0-0	-	1	0	0	2
Ron Harris	1	0-0	0-0	-	0	0	0	0
Wes Wallace	1	0-1	0-1	-	0	0	0	0
David Moss	12	0-1	0-0	-	1	1	0	0
TOTALS		FGM-A	FTM-A	OFF	REB	AST	PF	PTS
		29-60	6-10	-	25	15	18	64

March 15

Houston, TX

11. Boston College 55

6. Texas Tech 53

One of the great 3-point shooters in NBA history, Michael Adams gave a hint of things to come with one of the most clutch 2-pointers of the 1985 tournament. The diminutive guard sank a 25-footer with five seconds left to produce the upset victory for the Eagles.

Boston College, which used a stall to eat up almost all of the remaining 1:30 after Texas Tech's Vince Taylor had tied the score with a layup, put the ball in the hands of its best player with 13 seconds left after a time out. Adams maneuvered to the top of the key and hoisted one of his patented "push" shots that swished and broke the hearts of the large contingent of Red Raiders fans.

The thrilling victory did much to silence those who complained about the Eagles' inclusion in the field of 64. After all, Boston College had lost four straight heading into the postseason, and its roster of no-name, vertically-challenged scrappers seemed ill-equipped for a long March run. "I think we've been a good team all along," Eagles coach Gary Williams retorted. "Our games in the Big East Conference get us ready for the NCAA."

Adams, who finished with 17 points, was certainly ready for his small-ball showdown with Tech's Bubba Jennings, also 5-10, who was the Southwest Conference MVP. Jennings scored 16 points for the 17th-ranked Red Raiders, who had rolled into the tournament as the SWC regular-season and tourney champs on an 11-game winning streak.

TEXAS TECH RED RAIDERS

	MIN	FGM-A	FTM-A	OFF	REB	AST	PF	PTS
Quentin Anderson	-	1-5	4-4	-	5	0	1	6
Vince Taylor	-	6-9	0-0	-	12	1	3	12
Ray Irvin	-	3-6	1-2	-	8	0	3	7
Bubba Jennings	-	8-17	0-0	-	1	2	3	16
Phil Wallace	-	1-6	0-2	-	2	7	3	2
	MIN	FGM-A	FTM-A	OFF	REB	AST	PF	PTS
Tobin Doda	-	1-3	2-3	-	0	1	0	4
Dwight Phillips	-	0-1	0-0	-	1	0	1	0
Tony Benford	-	3-8	0-0	-	0	4	3	6
TOTALS		FGM-A	FTM-A	OFF	REB	AST	PF	PTS
		23-55	7-11	-	29	15	17	53

BOSTON COLLEGE EAGLES

	MIN	FGM-A	FTM-A	OFF	REB	AST	PF	PTS
Roger McCready	-	7-9	1-4	-	8	0	3	15
Terrence Talley	-	2-3	4-4	-	5	6	2	8
Trevor Gordon	-	0-3	2-6	-	6	0	2	2
Michael Adams	-	7-16	3-3	-	5	0	1	17
Dominic Pressley	-	1-3	1-2	-	1	1	4	3
	MIN	FGM-A	FTM-A	OFF	REB	AST	PF	PTS
Mark Schmidt	-	0-0	0-0	-	0	0	0	0
Stu Primus	-	2-4	3-4	-	2	1	2	7
Skip Barry	-	0-1	0-0	-	0	0	1	0
Troy Bowers	-	1-2	1-2	-	0	0	2	3
TOTALS		FGM-A	FTM-A	OFF	REB	AST	PF	PTS
		20-41	15-25	-	27	8	17	55

3. Duke 75
14. Pepperdine 62

Mike Krzyzewski's first-ever NCAA tournament victory came at the expense of another young up-and-comer who would soon become a champion. The Blue Devils blew open a close game in the second half to subdue a Pepperdine team coached by Jim Harrick, who would win the national title 10 years later with UCLA.

David Hendeson (15 points) and Johnny Dawkins (13) combined for 28 points after the break, almost equaling the Waves' output of 30, after the 10th-ranked Blue Devils entered the locker room with an uncomfortable 34-32 advantage.

It had been a topsy-turvy first 20 minutes, with Duke storming to a 10-2 lead only to see Pepperdine go ahead 28-21 behind Eric White, who made seven of eight first-half shots and finished with a game-high 26 points. The Blue Devils closed the half strong as Mark Alarie, playing with a painful hip pointer, spearheaded the offense before Henderson and Dawkins took over.

"Our playoff experience in the last two and one half years is starting to pay off," Coach K said of his dynasty in the making. "But Dawkins was the difference in the game."

DUKE BLUE DEVILS

	MIN	FGM-A	FTM-A	OFF	REB	AST	PF	PTS
Mark Alarie	31	7-11	2-2	1	9	1	1	16
Dan Meagher	29	3-6	0-0	1	8	3	2	6
Jay Bilas	20	3-6	1-3	1	3	1	4	7
Tommy Amaker	37	1-3	0-0	0	1	5	2	2
Johnny Dawkins	39	8-13	5-9	2	4	4	1	21
	MIN	FGM-A	FTM-A	OFF	REB	AST	PF	PTS
David Henderson	28	7-12	8-14	1	3	2	2	22
Kevin Strickland	6	0-1	0-0	1	1	1	1	0
Jay Bryan	1	0-0	1-2	0	1	0	1	1
Weldon Williams	2	0-0	0-0	0	0	0	0	0
Todd Anderson	1	0-0	0-0	0	0	0	1	0
Martin Nessley	2	0-0	0-0	0	0	0	1	0
Billy King	4	0-0	0-0	0	1	0	0	0
		FGM-A	FTM-A	OFF	REB	AST	PF	PTS
TOTALS		29-52	17-30	7	31	17	16	75

PEPPERDINE WAVES

	MIN	FGM-A	FTM-A	OFF	REB	AST	PF	PTS
Eric White	37	12-17	2-5	6	13	2	2	26

	MIN	FGM-A	FTM-A	OFF	REB	AST	PF	PTS
Anthony Frederick	28	2-9	0-0	3	9	1	5	4
Levy Middlebrooks	33	5-11	1-2	2	4	0	2	11
Jon Korfas	32	4-7	3-4	0	1	8	2	11
Dwayne Polee	32	2-11	1-2	2	2	2	5	5
	MIN	FGM-A	FTM-A	OFF	REB	AST	PF	PTS
Lamar Wilson	14	1-3	1-2	1	2	1	0	3
Joe Asberry	1	0-0	0-0	0	0	0	0	0
Artis Jones	1	0-0	0-0	0	0	0	0	0
Mike Mounts	1	0-0	0-0	0	0	0	1	0
Paul Conaway	1	0-0	0-0	0	0	0	0	0
Dave Brittain	20	1-3	0-1	0	3	1	3	2
TOTALS		FGM-A	FTM-A	OFF	REB	AST	PF	PTS
		27-61	8-16	14	34	15	20	62

7. Alabama-Birmingham 70
10. Michigan State 68

Michigan State might have had the best player, but that wasn't enough to defeat the better team. Sam Vincent's 32-point outburst failed to carry the Spartans past the Blazers, who benefitted from a controversial offensive goaltending call in the closing seconds to get their first NCAA tournament win in their fifth straight appearance.

Michigan State lost a basket with seven seconds left that would have cut its deficit to 69-68 when Ken Johnson was whistled for the infraction, a call which left coach Jud Heathcote livid after the game: "That same official called us in the lane on a free throw previously. That one guy is brutal. I don't even know his name and I don't want to."

Heathcote's counterpart, Gene Bartow, was just glad to have survived Vincent's dazzling performance. "Vincent was everything we were told," Bartow said. "We changed defenses four times in the second half to throw off their timing." The All-American, playing his final game, had led the Spartans to a 35-32 halftime lead with his 14 points on 6-of-9 shooting.

UAB, which got 18 points from both Steve Mitchell and Jerome Mincy, took the lead for good midway through the second half and held an 8-point advantage with 6:26 left before Michigan State rallied. But with a little help from a "nameless" official Bartow advanced to face his old team, Memphis State, whom he had guided to the Final Four a dozen years earlier.

ALABAMA-BIRMINGHAM BLAZERS								
	MIN	FGM-A	FTM-A	OFF	REB	AST	PF	PTS
Marvin Johnson	9	0-0	0-0	0	0	2	0	0
Jerome Mincy	37	6-15	6-13	4	7	0	2	18

	MIN	FGM-A	FTM-A	OFF	REB	AST	PF	PTS
Anthony Gordon	7	0-0	0-1	0	0	0	2	0
Steve Mitchell	38	8-12	2-2	0	1	5	3	18
James Ponder	37	3-9	9-10	1	2	1	1	15
	MIN	FGM-A	FTM-A	OFF	REB	AST	PF	PTS
Tracy Foster	10	1-2	0-0	0	0	1	0	2
Murry Bartow	6	0-0	0-0	0	1	0	0	0
Michael Charles	21	2-4	3-4	1	5	2	3	7
Archie Johnson	35	4-6	2-4	6	10	1	1	10
TOTALS		FGM-A	FTM-A	OFF	REB	AST	PF	PTS
		24-48	22-34	12	26	12	12	70

MICHIGAN STATE SPARTANS

	MIN	FGM-A	FTM-A	OFF	REB	AST	PF	PTS
Richard Mudd	23	1-4	0-0	4	8	0	5	2
Larry Polec	35	4-7	0-0	1	3	0	5	8
Ken Johnson	37	4-8	1-1	5	11	1	4	9
Scott Skiles	39	6-13	3-4	1	4	8	4	15
Sam Vincent	39	13-23	6-6	4	6	2	3	32
	MIN	FGM-A	FTM-A	OFF	REB	AST	PF	PTS
Darryl Johnson	24	1-5	0-0	1	1	4	2	2
Ralph Walker	2	0-0	0-0	0	0	0	2	0
Gregory Pedro	1	0-0	0-0	0	0	0	0	0
TOTALS		FGM-A	FTM-A	OFF	REB	AST	PF	PTS
		29-60	10-11	16	33	15	25	68

2. Memphis State 67
15. Pennsylvania 55

Underdog Penn seemed to do everything right against fifth-ranked Mempis State, except when it came to doing nothing at all. The Quakers considered using a stall tactic when they held a five-point lead in the second half but decided against it, and that gave the slumbering Tigers the opening they needed to avoid the colossal upset.

"If it had gotten down to, say, seven minutes, we would have," Penn coach Craig Littlepage said of stalling. "But 13 minutes to go was too long."

That was just fine with Memphis State, which used its press to harass the Quakers into a flurry of mistakes that were converted into easy baskets during a 23-4 spurt that left the Tigers with a comfortable 61-43 lead on the way to what would be a misleading final score.

The Ivy League champion Quakers, a 17-point underdog whose 13-14 record caused many to say they had no business being in the tournament, were the better team for most of the game. They collapsed on the Tigers' talented trio of big men – All-American Keith Lee, William Bedford and Baskerville Holmes – and dared the Metro Conference winners to hurt them from the outside. When Lee left after picking up his fourth foul early in the second half (he would not return), Penn's impossible dream began looking like reality.

But the loss of Lee might have been the break Memphis State needed. The Tigers, playing a smaller lineup, turned to a full-court press that caught the Quakers off-guard and turned the game around. Star guard Andre Turner, who finished with 16 points, led the charge, and Bedford snapped out of his funk to score all 11 of his points after intermission.

"We wanted to make them play 94 feet. Our defense keyed our offense," Turner said. Tigers coach Dana Kirk added, "I told our team at halftime they were sleepwalking. I told the team to play our music at our rhythm."

MEMPHIS STATE TIGERS

	MIN	FGM-A	FTM-A	OFF	REB	AST	PF	PTS
Keith Lee	20	4-8	0-2	1	3	0	4	8
Baskerville Holmes	36	3-6	2-3	3	7	1	2	8
William Bedford	29	5-5	1-4	3	8	0	3	11
Andre Turner	36	8-14	0-0	2	3	8	4	16
Vincent Askew	32	6-10	0-0	3	5	3	0	12
	MIN	FGM-A	FTM-A	OFF	REB	AST	PF	PTS
Ricky McCoy	4	0-0	3-4	0	2	0	0	3
John Wilfong	5	0-1	1-2	0	0	0	0	1
Dwight Boyd	19	2-6	0-0	2	3	5	1	4
Dewayne Bailey	4	0-0	2-2	0	1	0	1	2
David Jensen	2	0-1	0-0	0	0	0	0	0
Willie Becton	13	1-2	0-0	0	0	2	1	2
TOTALS		FGM-A	FTM-A	OFF	REB	AST	PF	PTS
		29-53	9-17	14	32	19	16	67

PENNSYLVANIA QUAKERS

	MIN	FGM-A	FTM-A	OFF	REB	AST	PF	PTS
Tyrone Pitts	32	5-7	2-2	1	3	0	4	12
Bruce Lefkowitz	27	2-6	3-4	3	8	3	2	7
Neil Bernstein	28	0-0	0-1	0	2	0	4	0
Perry Bromwell	36	6-11	4-4	0	2	1	1	16
Karl Racine	32	4-5	0-1	0	1	6	1	8

	MIN	FGM-A	FTM-A	OFF	REB	AST	PF	PTS
John Wilson	2	0-0	0-0	0	0	0	2	0
Chris Elzey	21	2-7	0-0	1	2	2	2	4
Rick Maloney	9	1-1	0-1	2	3	1	1	2
Scott Mascioli	1	3-3	0-0	1	2	0	1	6
Anthony Arnoli	9	0-1	0-0	0	0	0	1	0
Richard Cohan	1	0-1	0-0	1	2	0	0	0
Chris Borrillo	1	0-0	0-0	0	0	0	1	0
Keith Widmer	1	0-0	0-0	0	1	0	0	0
TOTALS		FGM-A	FTM-A	OFF	REB	AST	PF	PTS
		23-42	9-13	9	26	13	20	55

Second Round

East Region

March 16

Hartford, CT

1. Georgetown 63

8. Temple 46

For a few moments, at least, it appeared that Temple had a chance. Granger Hall and Ed Coe hit two quick shots to give the Owls both a 4-0 lead and hope that they could actually upset the top team in the country.

But then the Hoyas turned on the defensive intensity in the paint and bullied John Chaney's bunch from Philadelphia with another display of Georgetown might. Temple made only 39 percent of its shots and frontcourt stars Hall and Charles Rayne, who averaged a combined 31.2 points per game in 1984-85, were limited to a total of 15 as the Hoyas cut off the lane and forced the Owls to play from the outside.

Said Chaney, who before the game presented an apple to counterpart John Thompson for being the best "teacher" in college hoops: "If a team is going to double down on you, you have to take shots from the outside. We figured every time we'd get it to Granger, they'd double down on him." Or, as Michael Jackson, the Hoyas' top scorer on the day with 14 points, put it: "Because we knew who their money players are, we were able to cheat a little."

Georgetown was typically balanced in winning its 14th straight game. Reggie Williams scored 13 points and Patrick Ewing and David Wingate each had 12 as the Hoyas efficiently made 55 percent of their limited number of shots (38). After building an eight-point halftime advantage, the defending national champs started the second half with seven straight points while holding Temple scoreless for five minutes. The Owls later managed to trim a 16-point deficit in half, but the Hoyas were never seriously threatened as they advanced to the Sweet 16 in Providence, R.I.

"It's our time of year," backup Ralph Dalton declared. "This game was another game on the way to where we're going."

GEORGETOWN HOYAS								
	MIN	FGM-A	FTM-A	OFF	REB	AST	PF	PTS
Bill Martin	36	2-9	2-5	2	3	0	2	6
Reggie Williams	35	3-7	7-8	3	6	5	4	13
Patrick Ewing	36	4-6	4-7	1	7	1	4	12
Michael Jackson	33	6-7	2-3	0	1	5	3	14
David Wingate	32	3-5	6-8	2	3	2	4	12
	MIN	FGM-A	FTM-A	OFF	REB	AST	PF	PTS
Perry McDonald	4	0-0	0-0	0	0	0	0	0
Horace Broadnax	11	0-0	0-1	0	1	1	0	0
Ralph Dalton	11	3-4	0-1	0	1	0	1	6
Grady Mateen	1	0-0	0-0	1	2	0	1	0
Tyrone Lockhart	1	0-0	0-0	0	0	0	0	0
TOTALS		FGM-A	FTM-A	OFF	REB	AST	PF	PTS
		21-38	21-33	9	24	14	19	63

TEMPLE OWLS								
	MIN	FGM-A	FTM-A	OFF	REB	AST	PF	PTS
Granger Hall	21	2-4	3-5	0	3	1	4	7
Charles Rayne	39	2-9	2-2	3	7	1	5	6
Tim Perry	31	0-1	0-1	2	2	0	2	0
Nate Blackwell	39	5-12	5-5	2	2	3	5	15
Ed Coe	24	4-7	2-3	0	2	1	4	10
	MIN	FGM-A	FTM-A	OFF	REB	AST	PF	PTS
Derrick Brantley	12	1-2	0-1	2	3	0	3	2
Howard Evans	30	3-9	0-0	1	1	6	3	6
Kevin Clifton	1	0-0	0-0	0	0	0	1	0
Mark Poplawski	1	0-0	0-0	0	0	0	0	0
Shawn Johnson	1	0-0	0-0	0	0	0	0	0
Dwight Forrester	1	0-0	0-0	0	0	0	0	0
TOTALS		FGM-A	FTM-A	OFF	REB	AST	PF	PTS
		17-44	12-17	10	20	12	27	46

4. Loyola (IL) 70
5. SMU 57

Loyola's ironmen ran the nation's longest winning streak to 19 games, but all they could talk about was the mountain that loomed ahead.

"It will be power and speed vs. our speed," point guard Carl Golston said of the Ramblers' Sweet 16 foe, the Georgetown Hoyas. "Georgetown has all the advantages, but this year it will be our turn to be giant killers."

Golston had reason for his optimism based on Loyola's impressive dismantling of the bigger Mustangs from SMU despite an off game from superstar Alfredrick Hughes, the nation's leading scorer at 27.3 points per game, who was held to just 14. The Ramblers advanced thanks to their tireless starting lineup. Four of Loyola's five starters played 39 of the game's 40 minutes, and the fifth was in for 31 minutes.

"They run pretty well. They just decided not to. That probably helped us out a lot," Loyola coach Gene Sullivan said. "They (the Ramblers) like to play. It's hard to get them out of the game."

Helping Loyola's cause was SMU's unusual lack of fire. "For some reason, I thought that we were a very flat basketball team today," said Mustangs coach Dave Bliss, whose team was playing for a rematch with Georgetown, which survived SMU 37-36 in the '84 tournament. "We didn't get the job done offensively." Indeed, take away Jon Koncak's 8-of-12 shooting and SMU made only 38 percent of its attempts.

Still, the Mustangs led for most of the first half before the Ramblers rallied for a one-point lead at halftime, and Loyola's advantage was just six with 7:30 remaining when SMU slipped into the offensive funk that Bliss noted. The Mustangs went scoreless for five minutes as the Ramblers built a comfortable 63-50 cushion and cruised to victory.

SMU MUSTANGS								
	MIN	FGM-A	FTM-A	OFF	REB	AST	PF	PTS
Reginald Pink	13	0-2	0-0	0	1	0	0	0
Larry Davis	31	7-13	0-0	4	9	0	2	14
Jon Koncak	32	8-12	3-4	2	10	2	3	19
Butch Moore	30	1-4	0-0	2	6	9	5	2
Carl Wright	36	6-16	1-2	2	4	5	3	13
	MIN	FGM-A	FTM-A	OFF	REB	AST	PF	PTS
Kevin Lewis	18	1-2	0-0	1	4	1	2	2
Johnny Fuller	11	1-1	0-0	0	0	2	3	2
Terry Williams	17	2-8	1-2	3	7	1	1	5
Scott Johnson	12	0-1	0-0	0	1	0	0	0
TOTALS		FGM-A	FTM-A	OFF	REB	AST	PF	PTS

		26-59	5-8	14	42	21	19	57

LOYOLA (IL) RAMBLERS

	MIN	FGM-A	FTM-A	OFF	REB	AST	PF	PTS
Alfredrick Hughes	39	7-19	0-0	2	6	1	3	14
Andre Battle	31	5-13	2-3	1	3	2	3	12
Andre Moore	39	3-9	2-3	6	10	0	3	8
Greg Williams	39	4-7	2-2	2	4	7	2	10
Carl Golston	39	6-14	8-10	0	4	5	1	20
	MIN	FGM-A	FTM-A	OFF	REB	AST	PF	PTS
Mike Cenar	9	2-4	0-0	2	3	0	0	4
Bobby Clark	1	0-0	0-0	0	0	1	0	0
Ivan Young	1	0-1	0-0	0	0	0	1	0
Dave Klusendorf	1	1-1	0-0	0	0	0	0	2
Nate Brooks	1	0-0	0-0	0	1	0	0	0
TOTALS		FGM-A	FTM-A	OFF	REB	AST	PF	PTS
		28-68	14-18	13	31	16	13	70

March 17
Atlanta
3. Illinois 74
6. Georgia 58

One tenacious zone defense plus one long scoring spurt equaled one surprisingly easy win for the 12th-ranked Fighting Illini.

Illinois frustrated Georgia all game with its defense and all but sealed the victory with a 16-0 run midway through the first half that turned a 16-15 toss-up into a 32-15 laugher. "We were in the game when it was 16-15, then it was Illinois the rest of the way," Bulldogs coach Hugh Durham said.

Illini coach Lou Henson's decision to ignore his own game plan might have been the key to his team's rout. "We had planned to alternate our defense and use the zone to keep us out of foul trouble," Henson said. "But when Georgia struggled with the outside shot, we decided to stay with the zone."

Point guard Bruce Douglas was the key to Illinois' defensive effort. He produced six steals and helped set up several easy fast-break layups with his in-your-face defense on the perimeter. Douglas' backcourt partner, Doug Altenberger, torched the Dawgs with 8 of his 16 points during Illinois' decisive first-half run that saw Georgia go scoreless for 9:12 as their large fan turnout sat in silence.

Illinois led 34-19 at halftime and increased its margin to 22 by scoring the first 7 points in the second half. Twice the 19th-ranked Bulldogs cut the deficit to 10 but the Illini, the only one of the Big Ten's six teams to survive the tournament's opening week, were never seriously threatened.

GEORGIA BULLDOGS

	MIN	FGM-A	FTM-A	OFF	REB	AST	PF	PTS
Richard Corhen	18	1-2	0-0	-	2	0	4	2
Joe Ward	24	7-15	3-3	-	3	3	2	17
Cedric Henderson	33	5-14	3-4	-	5	0	4	13
Gerald Crosby	37	4-9	0-0	-	2	6	1	8
Donald Hartry	19	0-2	0-0	-	1	4	0	0
	MIN	FGM-A	FTM-A	OFF	REB	AST	PF	PTS
Melvin Howard	21	1-3	1-2	-	1	2	3	3
Chad Kessler	11	2-3	0-0	-	2	0	0	4
Horace McMillan	16	1-4	0-3	-	3	0	1	2
David Dunn	18	3-3	1-1	-	7	0	3	7
Dennis Williams	3	1-1	0-0	-	0	0	0	2
TOTALS		FGM-A	FTM-A	OFF	REB	AST	PF	PTS
		25-56	8-13	-	26	15	18	58

ILLINOIS FIGHTING ILLINI

	MIN	FGM-A	FTM-A	OFF	REB	AST	PF	PTS
Ken Norman	37	7-11	1-2	-	9	0	0	15
Anthony Welch	34	4-8	0-0	-	3	3	0	8
Efrem Winters	25	6-9	7-7	-	5	0	5	19
Doug Altenberger	35	7-10	2-2	-	4	1	2	16
Bruce Douglas	39	2-9	1-2	-	9	11	2	5
	MIN	FGM-A	FTM-A	OFF	REB	AST	PF	PTS
Scott Meents	10	1-3	0-0	-	1	2	3	2
Tony Wysinger	16	2-3	3-4	-	1	1	3	7
Scott Haffner	2	1-2	0-0	-	0	0	0	2
Reggie Woodward	2	0-0	0-0	-	0	1	0	0
TOTALS		FGM-A	FTM-A	OFF	REB	AST	PF	PTS
		30-55	14-17	-	32	19	15	74

2. Georgia Tech 70

7. Syracuse 53

Size did matter on this day for Georgia Tech. Yvon Joseph and John Salley, both 7-footers, reigned in the paint on both ends of the floor as the ACC champion Yellow Jackets used a big second half to trounce the Orangemen.

Joseph scored 17 points and Salley produced 10 of his 13 points in a second half that saw Tech turn a 28-27 halftime lead into a 17-point blowout. "I'm proud of our big people," Yellow Jacket coach Bobby Cremins said. "It was our big guys. It was an unbelievable win. The score was no indication of the game."

Syracuse coach Jim Boeheim also sang Joseph's praises: "The big guy Joseph hurt us inside the whole game. They pushed us outside and just played excellent team defense." And Tech's star guard Mark Price, who led all scorers with 18 points, joined the chorus, although he got a little ahead of himself: "I thought Yvon Joseph won this tournament for us. He shot the ball well both games."

Georgia Tech's two giants, along with Bruce Dalrymple (10 rebounds), helped the Jackets take a 38-24 edge in rebounds while holding Orangemen freshman center Rony Seikaly to just 8 points. Syracuse All-Big East guard Dwayne "Pearl" Washington also had an off day, finishing with 7 points on 2-of-9 shooting.

The Yellow Jackets would now have to leave the friendly confines of Atlanta's Omni, where they had won their last five games (three in the ACC tournament and two in the NCAA tourney). But with the middle manned by Salley and the 27-year-old Haitian Joseph ("I've never played anybody as big and strong as (him)", Oklahoma's Wayman Tisdale said of him), the Final Four seemed within reach.

SYRACUSE ORANGEMEN

	MIN	FGM-A	FTM-A	OFF	REB	AST	PF	PTS
Rafael Addison	40	6-13	5-6	-	5	1	4	17
Andre Hawkins	11	1-4	0-0	-	2	0	2	2
Rony Seikaly	32	3-8	2-4	-	5	0	3	8
Dwayne Washington	38	2-9	3-4	-	2	11	4	7
Melvin Brown	30	4-9	0-0	-	3	1	4	8
	MIN	FGM-A	FTM-A	OFF	REB	AST	PF	PTS
Wendall Alexis	33	5-8	1-2	-	4	0	5	11
Greg Monroe	13	0-1	0-0	-	1	1	1	0
Herman Harried	3	0-1	0-1	-	1	0	1	0
TOTALS		FGM-A	FTM-A	OFF	REB	AST	PF	PTS
		21-53	11-17	-	23	14	24	53

GEORGIA TECH YELLOW JACKETS

	MIN	FGM-A	FTM-A	OFF	REB	AST	PF	PTS
John Salley	40	5-8	3-6	-	9	2	3	13
Scott Petway	36	2-5	4-4	-	7	2	4	8
Yvon Joseph	36	4-8	9-10	-	5	3	2	17
Mark Price	40	6-14	6-6	-	3	2	2	18
Bruce Dalrymple	36	3-7	4-5	-	10	6	5	10
	MIN	FGM-A	FTM-A	OFF	REB	AST	PF	PTS

		FGM-A	FTM-A	OFF	REB	AST	PF	PTS
Antoine Ford	4	0-1	0-0	-	0	0	0	0
Duane Farrell	7	1-2	0-0	-	1	2	0	2
Jack Mansell	1	0-0	2-2	-	2	0	0	2
TOTALS		FGM-A	FTM-A	OFF	REB	AST	PF	PTS
		21-45	28-33	-	37	17	16	70

West Region

March 16
Salt Lake City, UT
1. St. John's 68
9. Arkansas 65

If only Arkansas could figure out how to contain Chris Mullin, they might have pulled off one of the biggest shockers in NCAA tournament history. And perhaps Mullin, who finished with 26 points, would have been managed if Razorbacks coach Eddie Sutton had not chosen to put 6-2 guard Allie Freeman on the 6-6 All-American.

As it was, Arkansas still trailed only 62-61 with 1:32 remaining, but two Redmen free throws followed by a clutch blocked shot by center Bill Wennington helped the third-ranked power from the Big East avert the upset. "Bill did a heck of a job," St. John's coach Lou Carnesecca said. "We had the big guy (Arkansas center Joe Kleine) in jail all day, and he still got 23 points. We took a calculated risk and did a pretty good job of keeping the ball away from him."

St. John's strategy was to sag on Kleine, who was an Olympic teammate of Mullin in 1984, and force the Razorbacks to win from the perimeter. The ploy worked beautifully in the first half, as Kleine was limited to seven points and the Redmen enjoyed a 32-26 halftime advantage. Kleine erupted in the second half but could do little more than match Mullin's production.

"Against most teams in the NCAA field, we probably played well enough to win. But not today," Sutton said. "The more you play the game, the slower the game becomes. You learn shortcuts. Chris (Mullin) is as smart as I've seen."

The game would be Sutton's last as Arkansas' coach. Two weeks after telling the Arkansas Legislature that he wanted to stay a Razorback until he retired, Sutton accepted the Kentucky job during the Final Four, saying "I would have crawled all the way to Lexington" and "this is where I belong". Four years later, he would be run out of the Bluegrass State thanks to a scandal that almost resulted in the school getting the NCAA's dreaded "death penalty".

ST. JOHN'S REDMEN								
	MIN	FGM-A	FTM-A	OFF	REB	AST	PF	PTS
Walter Berry	40	6-11	4-5	-	6	0	3	16
Willie Glass	32	4-5	1-2	-	4	2	2	9

	MIN	FGM-A	FTM-A	OFF	REB	AST	PF	PTS
Bill Wennington	33	3-4	1-2	-	9	0	3	7
Chris Mullin	40	8-15	10-10	-	5	4	4	26
Mike Moses	32	2-4	4-5	-	2	5	1	8
	MIN	FGM-A	FTM-A	OFF	REB	AST	PF	PTS
Mark Jackson	8	0-0	2-4	-	0	1	0	2
Shelton Jones	8	0-0	0-0	-	1	1	1	0
Ron Stewart	7	0-0	0-0	-	0	0	1	0
TOTALS		FGM-A	FTM-A	OFF	REB	AST	PF	PTS
		23-39	22-28	-	27	13	15	68

ARKANSAS RAZORBACKS

	MIN	FGM-A	FTM-A	OFF	REB	AST	PF	PTS
William Mills	30	6-15	0-0	-	0	4	3	12
Charles Balentine	40	4-8	0-1	-	5	4	3	8
Joe Kleine	40	7-15	9-10	-	11	1	4	23
Kenny Hutchinson	25	2-3	0-0	-	3	3	5	4
Allie Freeman	34	5-7	1-2	-	1	0	5	11
	MIN	FGM-A	FTM-A	OFF	REB	AST	PF	PTS
Scott Rose	2	0-0	0-0	-	0	1	1	0
Kevin Rehl	1	1-1	0-0	-	0	0	1	2
Byron Irvin	18	2-6	1-2	-	3	4	2	5
Andrew Lang	6	0-0	0-0	-	1	0	0	0
Eric Poerschke	4	0-1	0-0	-	1	0	0	0
TOTALS		FGM-A	FTM-A	OFF	REB	AST	PF	PTS
		27-56	11-15	-	25	17	24	65

12. Kentucky 64
4. UNLV 61

Kentucky coach Joe B. Hall once called star forward Kenny Walker "the greatest player in America today". Walker lived up to Hall's lofty praise in leading the Wildcats to their second major upset in three days while ensuring that the coach would stick around the storied program for at least one more game.

Walker's 23-point effort was highlighted by one pivotal sequence of events. With Kentucky leading 60-59, "Sky" Walker went high to reject a Richie Adams shot and then raced down the court for a layup with 21 seconds left that helped seal the victory. Walker's heroics came after the Wildcats had wasted almost all of a 60-52 advantage with 4:49 remaining thanks to three consecutive turnovers when they were trying to run out the clock.

"He's made plays like that blocked shot all year long," Hall said. "When you need a great play, he'll get it for you." The Kentucky coach deserved some credit, too, for deploying a zone defense that slowed the game down and helped limit the run-and-gun Rebels to 21 points below their season average.

Hall, who was facing rumors that he would quit or be fired by the school after a 16-12 regular season ("I had to hold myself from packing my bags and getting out of town"), was carried off the floor by his players after the win. "We never doubted for a minute we belonged in this tournament, and the critics who said we shouldn't be gave us some added incentive," Hall said.

Kentucky's unusual Cinderella role also suited Walker just fine. "Now we're going to Denver with momentum, because now we know we can win," the All-American said. If the Cats could keep doing the improbable, their reward would be a Final Four on their home floor at Rupp Arena.

KENTUCKY WILDCATS

	MIN	FGM-A	FTM-A	OFF	REB	AST	PF	PTS
Winston Bennett	-	1-2	2-2	-	4	2	3	4
Kenny Walker	-	10-14	3-5	-	6	1	1	23
Bret Bearup	-	0-2	2-2	-	1	3	1	2
Ed Davender	-	6-10	1-2	-	4	1	0	13
Roger Harden	-	4-6	0-0	-	1	6	3	8
	MIN	FGM-A	FTM-A	OFF	REB	AST	PF	PTS
James Blackmon	-	2-6	0-0	-	2	2	0	4
Richard Madison	-	2-4	3-3	-	3	0	0	7
Robert Lock	-	0-1	1-2	-	1	0	1	1
Cedric Jenkins	-	1-2	0-0	-	2	0	1	2
TOTALS		FGM-A	FTM-A	OFF	REB	AST	PF	PTS
		26-47	12-16	-	24	15	10	64

UNLV REBELS

	MIN	FGM-A	FTM-A	OFF	REB	AST	PF	PTS
Frank James	28	5-8	0-0	-	1	5	0	10
Armon Gilliam	21	3-3	0-0	-	1	0	3	6
Richie Adams	34	6-14	2-2	-	13	1	3	14
Anthony Jones	35	6-14	1-1	-	4	4	1	13
Freddie Banks	27	4-8	0-0	-	1	2	5	8
	MIN	FGM-A	FTM-A	OFF	REB	AST	PF	PTS
Richard Robinson	17	0-3	2-2	-	2	0	2	2
Ed Catchings	20	4-6	0-1	-	2	3	2	8
Gary Graham	13	0-1	0-0	-	0	2	1	0
Eldridge Hudson	5	0-1	0-0	-	0	0	1	0
TOTALS		FGM-A	FTM-A	OFF	REB	AST	PF	PTS

| 28-58 | 5-6 | - | 24 | 17 | 18 | 61 |

March 17
Albuquerque, NM
3. North Carolina State 86
11. UTEP 73

"I was concerned about coming back here," North Carolina State coach Jim Valvano said of playing at The Pit. It turned out he had nothing to be worried about. After easily dispatching Nevada-Reno in the opening round, the Wolfpack had little trouble adjusting to UTEP's up-tempo style as they completed a two-game sweep in their return to the site of their 1983 championship.

"What could you do to top winning a championship?" Valvano asked after the game. "What we had to do was win two games and we did, and I'm glad we didn't tarnish what we did in 1983."

One of the heroes of '83, Lorenzo Charles, had a big hand in creating some new happy Albuquerque memories. Charles, playing farther away from the basket than normal, scored 30 points in leading the Pack to a sizzling 73 percent shooting day from the floor, which was an NCAA tournament record for a first- or second-round game.

The Miners' second big thorn was actually a little one – 5-foot-7 Spud Webb. The bug of a point guard finished with a career-high 29 points, 23 of them in the second half when N.C. State turned a 3-point halftime lead into a blowout. Webb was masterful at protecting the ball and finding open shots for himself. "He was what hurt us," lamented UTEP senior Kent Lockhart.

While his second visit to The Pit might not have been as special as his first, it still was a rewarding return for Valvano. "It's like going back to a high school class reunion where all of a sudden your best friend is fat and bald," the happy coach quipped. "I didn't want to be fat and bald."

NORTH CAROLINA STATE WOLF PACK							
	MIN	FGM-A	FTM-A	OFF REB	AST	PF	PTS
Russell Pierre	17	2-4	3-6	- 9	0	3	7
Mike Warren	1	0-0	0-0	- 0	0	0	0
Lorenzo Charles	38	12-15	6-10	- 10	0	3	30
Spud Webb	37	8-9	13-17	- 2	7	3	29
Cozell McQueen	40	2-3	0-0	- 3	0	2	4
	MIN	FGM-A	FTM-A	OFF REB	AST	PF	PTS
Bennie Bolton	19	2-3	1-2	- 2	0	2	5
Terry Gannon	7	0-1	0-0	- 1	1	1	0
Quentin Jackson	1	0-0	0-0	- 0	0	0	0
Nate McMillan	31	3-3	3-5	- 3	5	4	9
Ernie Myers	9	1-3	0-0	- 2	1	1	2

TOTALS		FGM-A	FTM-A	OFF	REB	AST	PF	PTS
		30-41	26-40	-	32	14	19	86

UTEP MINERS								
	MIN	FGM-A	FTM-A	OFF	REB	AST	PF	PTS
Donnell Allen	18	2-3	4-4	-	0	0	2	8
Kevin Hamilton	20	0-1	0-0	-	0	0	1	0
Marvin Washington	1	0-0	0-0	-	0	0	1	0
Lemuel Clanton	2	0-1	0-0	-	0	0	2	0
Jamaal Smith	38	3-12	4-6	-	5	1	4	10
	MIN	FGM-A	FTM-A	OFF	REB	AST	PF	PTS
Quintan Gates	15	2-4	1-1	-	2	0	1	5
Dave Feitl	26	5-9	2-3	-	7	2	4	12
Kent Lockhart	32	4-11	2-2	-	2	1	5	10
Jeep Jackson	10	3-5	0-0	-	2	3	4	6
Luster Goodwin	38	9-15	4-4	-	0	2	5	22
TOTALS		FGM-A	FTM-A	OFF	REB	AST	PF	PTS
		28-61	17-20	-	18	9	29	73

7. Alabama 63
2. Virginia Commonwealth 59

Upstart Virginia Commonwealth played less like a No. 2 seed and more like a squad uncomfortable with the spotlight and high expectations. The 11th-ranked Rams were held without a field goal for the final 9:10 of the first half as Alabama ground out an upset win that was its ninth in the last 10 games.

The Crimson Tide turned an early four-point deficit into a 31-17 advantage thanks to the Rams' inability to shoot straight after Bama coach Wimp Sanderson switched to a 3-2 zone defense. "I thought they were going to play man-to-man the whole game," said a disappointed Rolando Lamb, who still managed to score 25 points in his final game. "Yeah, the 3-2 surprised me. That turned the game around for them."

"It's very obvious that we can't win shooting 42 percent," added VCU coach J.D. Barnett. "I'm feeling very empty." A mentor to Tubby Smith, Barnett would leave the school after this loss to take the head coaching position at Tulsa.

Bobby Lee Hurt paced the Crimson Tide with 19 points and 13 rebounds, but it was his defense at the heart of the zone that perhaps was the game's biggest key. Hurt and Buck Johnson combined to block seven shots and totally cut off the lane for the Rams.

"Bobby Lee played a lot better than he had been playing," Tide coach Wimp Sanderson noted. "He boarded aggressively and he shot the inside shot very well."

VCU clawed back to within 51-47 with 3:40 left. But Alabama's Mark Gottfried sank two foul shots and then Hurt crushed the Rams with a crucial 3-point play with just under three minutes remaining.

The victory was bittersweet for one of Sanderson's assistants. Benny Dees was the first coach of VCU when the school started its basketball program in 1968 and guided the team for two years before he had to leave after his father's death to take over the family farm. Dees would get a second crack at head coaching after Bama's run to the Sweet 16, taking over at New Orleans before heading to Wyoming, where his 1988 team was upset in the first round by Hank Gathers, Bo Kimble and run-and-gun Loyola Marymount.

ALABAMA CRIMSON TIDE

	MIN	FGM-A	FTM-A	OFF	REB	AST	PF	PTS
Darrell Neal	9	0-1	0-1	-	2	0	3	0
Terry Coner	37	5-7	4-6	-	1	5	3	14
Jim Farmer	24	4-10	0-2	-	2	0	1	8
Derrick McKey	35	3-7	0-1	-	3	3	2	6
Buck Johnson	35	1-5	4-5	-	10	2	3	6
	MIN	FGM-A	FTM-A	OFF	REB	AST	PF	PTS
Mark Gottfried	20	3-8	4-4	-	2	0	2	10
Bobby Lee Hurt	40	8-10	3-4	-	13	0	2	19
TOTALS		FGM-A	FTM-A	OFF	REB	AST	PF	PTS
		24-48	15-22	-	33	10	16	63

VIRGINIA COMMONWEALTH RAMS

	MIN	FGM-A	FTM-A	OFF	REB	AST	PF	PTS
Bruce Allen	1	0-0	0-0	-	0	0	0	0
Neil Wake	22	0-1	1-3	-	7	0	2	1
Alvin Robinson	5	0-0	0-0	-	0	0	1	0
Mike Schlegel	40	7-12	1-3	-	8	2	4	15
Phil Stinnie	2	0-0	0-0	-	0	0	0	0
	MIN	FGM-A	FTM-A	OFF	REB	AST	PF	PTS
Robert Dickerson	14	1-2	0-0	-	0	0	5	2
Michael Brown	40	2-9	1-2	-	4	1	3	5
Rolando Lamb	39	12-23	1-2	-	7	3	5	25
Calvin Duncan	37	5-16	1-3	-	8	1	5	11
TOTALS		FGM-A	FTM-A	OFF	REB	AST	PF	PTS
		27-63	5-13	-	34	7	25	59

Southeast Region

March 16
South Bend, IN
11. Auburn 66
3. Kansas 64

If Sonny Smith didn't already have second thoughts about leaving his job as Auburn coach, then the Tigers' unlikely run to the Sweet 16 might have done the trick. Many expected that this would be Smith's final game, but thanks to the clutch scoring of Chuck Person and Frank Ford and an unusually poor day for Kansas stars Danny Manning and Greg Dreiling, Smith's planned departure was delayed.

"I said to this team, if you can get to Birmingham (site of the regional finals), the sky's the limit," Smith said. "I think this bunch can get there with a team that shouldn't get there."

The Tigers almost didn't get there thanks to severe foul trouble, most notably Person, who played much of the second half with four fouls but still managed to finish with 21 points. "He (Person) had to play with four fouls and he still came up with some great plays," Smith said. Ford, a role player who saw extended action thanks to Person's foul issues, produced a game-high 23 points on perfect 9-for-9 shooting. "Frank refused to be beat," Smith added. "When you've got people like him, you never know what can happen."

Helping Auburn greatly was the 13th-ranked Jayhawks' own foul miseries. Manning spent a large part of the first half sitting on the bench as part of a poor game that saw him shoot 3 of 12 and score just 7 points to go along with the 7-foot-1 Dreiling's meager 2. Nevertheless, trailing 59-52 with 1:30 to play, Kansas nearly pulled off an improbable comeback, twice clawing within one point and finally missing a potential game-tying shot at the buzzer.

Even before the upset of Kansas, there were rumors that Smith would "un-resign" and stay at Auburn. Those rumors would become reality two weeks later when Smith announced that he had withdrawn his resignation.

KANSAS JAYHAWKS	MIN	FGM-A	FTM-A	OFF	REB	AST	PF	PTS
Mark Pellock	8	0-0	0-0	-	1	0	0	0
Chris Piper	20	3-4	0-0	-	1	1	3	6
Calvin Thompson	37	10-16	1-2	-	1	2	3	21
Milt Newton	4	0-1	0-0	-	1	0	0	0
Mark Turgeon	7	1-2	0-0	-	1	0	0	2
	MIN	FGM-A	FTM-A	OFF	REB	AST	PF	PTS
Thomas Boyle	2	0-0	0-0	-	0	0	0	0
Danny Manning	22	3-12	1-2	-	8	1	4	7
Ronald Kellogg	38	8-16	1-1	-	5	1	2	17

	MIN	FGM-A	FTM-A	OFF	REB	AST	PF	PTS
Greg Dreiling	29	1-4	0-0	-	6	0	4	2
Cedric Hunter	33	4-9	1-2	-	3	4	2	9
TOTALS		FGM-A	FTM-A	OFF	REB	AST	PF	PTS
		30-64	4-7	-	27	9	18	64

AUBURN TIGERS

	MIN	FGM-A	FTM-A	OFF	REB	AST	PF	PTS
Chuck Person	31	10-19	1-2	-	5	2	4	21
Gerald White	38	1-2	7-8	-	2	5	3	9
Frank Ford	37	9-9	5-6	-	7	1	3	23
Carey Holland	20	0-0	0-0	-	3	0	2	0
Johnny Lynn	5	0-0	0-0	-	0	0	0	0
	MIN	FGM-A	FTM-A	OFF	REB	AST	PF	PTS
Darren Guest	4	0-3	0-0	-	5	0	0	0
Jeff Moore	25	2-7	1-1	-	5	0	1	5
Chris Morris	40	4-9	0-1	-	4	1	1	8
TOTALS		FGM-A	FTM-A	OFF	REB	AST	PF	PTS
		26-49	14-18	-	31	9	14	66

2. North Carolina 60
7. Notre Dame 58

Did David Rivers dribble the ball off his foot, or did Chris Hunter take it from him? However it's interpreted, the Fighting Irish star's turnover with seconds left led to the winning basket in North Carolina's heart-stopping win.

Rivers, Notre Dame's point guard, was holding the ball for a game-ending shot when he lost it on the dribble. The Tar Heels' Hunter snatched it up and passed ahead to a streaking Kenny Smith, who laid it in with three seconds left to break the tie.

Rivers claimed after the game that the ball was slapped away, but Smith said, "I saw the ball go off his leg and I broke down the court. I thought maybe we'd get it, but not that way. I thought maybe we'd intercept a pass."

Irish coach Digger Phelps came under fire for leaving the freshman Rivers to his own devices instead of calling a timeout to set up a final play. "We'd been living with David all year. If I had the same opportunity again, Rivers would still have the ball and we'd make the same move," Phelps offered in his defense.

Smith wrapped up the Tar Heels' victory by deflecting Notre Dame's final inbounds pass, sending the Irish's South Bend home crowd to the exits in a foul mood, but not before they had witnessed a thrilling game that saw the Irish fight back from a late 6-point deficit to tie the game at 56. Notre Dame would soon even the score again at 58 on two Rivers free throws, but the Irish's unusually poor foul shooting (14 of 26 for a team that shot 75 percent for the season) proved just as fatal as Rivers' fateful turnover.

NORTH CAROLINA TAR HEELS

	MIN	FGM-A	FTM-A	OFF	REB	AST	PF	PTS
Buzz Peterson	36	3-5	1-3	-	2	2	1	7
Dave Popson	17	4-6	0-0	-	2	0	1	8
Brad Daugherty	31	6-8	6-6	-	12	2	4	18
Joe Wolf	38	3-7	0-0	-	6	0	4	6
Kenny Smith	40	6-11	0-2	-	2	5	3	12
	MIN	FGM-A	FTM-A	OFF	REB	AST	PF	PTS
Ranzino Smith	4	0-2	0-0	-	0	0	0	0
Warren Martin	26	3-5	1-1	-	5	2	5	7
Curtis Hunter	8	1-3	0-0	-	1	0	0	2
TOTALS		FGM-A	FTM-A	OFF	REB	AST	PF	PTS
		26-47	8-12	-	30	11	18	60

NOTRE DAME FIGHTING IRISH

	MIN	FGM-A	FTM-A	OFF	REB	AST	PF	PTS
Ken Barlow	27	4-9	0-2	-	3	0	3	8
Joseph Price	25	3-5	3-4	-	2	1	3	9
David Rivers	37	8-14	1-4	-	0	3	4	17
Scott Hicks	30	3-9	2-2	-	0	4	1	8
Donald Royal	38	1-3	6-10	-	5	2	0	8
	MIN	FGM-A	FTM-A	OFF	REB	AST	PF	PTS
Tim Kempton	20	1-3	2-2	-	4	0	3	4
Jim Dolan	20	2-2	0-2	-	6	0	4	4
Dan Duff	3	0-0	0-0	-	0	0	0	0
TOTALS		FGM-A	FTM-A	OFF	REB	AST	PF	PTS
		22-45	14-26	-	20	10	18	58

March 17
Dayton, OH
8. Villanova 59
1. Michigan 55

The "D-Train" was running at full speed and Cinderella-in-the-making Villanova was happy to ride him into the Sweet 16.

Dwayne "D-Train" McClain made 8 of 12 shots for a game-high 20 points and proved to be a key difference as the Wildcats shocked the Big Ten champs, ending the 2nd-ranked Wolverines' 17-game winning streak. "I was looking for my shot today more than the other night (first-round win over Dayton)," said McClain, who actually finished the Dayton game on a roll with 11 second-half points. "They were packing it in on Ed (Pinckney) and that was the shot they were giving us."

Perhaps an even bigger factor than McClain was Villanova's experience. The Wildcats, who started three seniors, kept their poise when they endured an 11-and-a-half minute stretch from late in the opening half until well into the second when no one, not even McClain, could find the basket. As a result of that epic field goal drought, 'Nova saw a six-point lead turn into a 35-30 deficit. Michigan failed to capitalize on its chance to blow out the Wildcats largely because offensive stars Roy Tarpley (only 2 of his 14 points in the second half) and Gary Grant (zero points for the game) were ice cold, too.

"I think their experience, six straight years in the tournament, helped," Wolverines coach Bill Frieder opined. "Veteran clubs are the ones that survive."

Villanova heated up again and, after a McClain jumper, held a 46-43 lead with four minutes remaining. The Cats' poise came through as they took advantage of the lack of a shot clock, expertly holding the ball and, when fouled, calmly draining free throw after free throw (25 of 31 for the game, including 14 of 16 down the stretch).

If nobody else was convinced that the Wildcats were in the midst of something special, McClain sure was. "We didn't come into this game thinking we were underdogs," he said. "When you reach this point in the tournament, you have to believe you can play with anybody."

MICHIGAN WOLVERINES

	MIN	FGM-A	FTM-A	OFF	REB	AST	PF	PTS
Roy Tarpley	40	7-14	0-0	-	13	1	1	14
Garde Thompson	18	3-5	2-3	-	1	2	2	8
Richard Rellford	28	5-7	1-2	-	2	0	4	11
Butch Wade	25	0-1	0-0	-	8	3	3	0
Leslie Rockymore	11	3-4	0-0	-	1	1	2	6
	MIN	FGM-A	FTM-A	OFF	REB	AST	PF	PTS
Antoine Joubert	30	6-13	0-0	-	1	3	5	12
Robert Henderson	15	2-3	0-0	-	2	1	1	4
Gary Grant	33	0-4	0-0	-	0	1	5	0
TOTALS		FGM-A	FTM-A	OFF	REB	AST	PF	PTS
		26-51	3-5	-	28	12	23	55

VILLANOVA WILDCATS

	MIN	FGM-A	FTM-A	OFF	REB	AST	PF	PTS
Ed Pinckney	40	2-4	10-11	-	7	1	2	14

	MIN	FGM-A	FTM-A	OFF	REB	AST	PF	PTS
Mark Plansky	9	1-1	2-2	-	1	1	1	4
Harold Pressley	34	3-10	3-5	-	7	2	3	9
Dwight Wilbur	15	0-2	0-0	-	0	1	1	0
Dwayne McClain	36	8-12	4-4	-	4	1	2	20
	MIN	FGM-A	FTM-A	OFF	REB	AST	PF	PTS
Chuck Everson	2	0-0	0-0	-	0	0	0	0
Harold Jensen	27	0-1	3-4	-	2	1	0	3
Gary McLain	37	3-5	3-5	-	0	3	2	9
TOTALS		FGM-A	FTM-A	OFF	REB	AST	PF	PTS
		17-35	25-31	-	21	10	11	59

5. Maryland 64
13. Navy 59

Two of the Washington, D.C. area's biggest stars had to travel to Dayton, Ohio to finally meet on the hardwood. When they dueled head-to-head in the game's final 20 minutes, it was Maryland's Len Bias who emerged as the winner over Navy's David Robinson.

Robinson had his way with the Terrapins in the first half, scoring 14 points and helping the Midshipmen amass a 37-32 halftime lead as they sought their second straight upset. But then Maryland coach Lefty Driesell made the game's key move, putting the 6-foot-8 Bias on the 6-11 "Admiral". Bias limited the future NBA superstar to 8 points in the second half, helping the Terps crawl out of a big hole.

"I tried to push him out farther from the basket," Bias said of Robinson. "When he's got the ball in the lane, it's as good as two points."

Still, Navy's lead grew to 45-34 before Maryland, led by Bias's 20 points, snapped back, ultimately taking a 58-57 lead with 4:30 remaining. The Middies then watched as the Terrapins stalled for four minutes before Jeff Adkins was sent to the line after a foul. Adkins coolly sank both ends of a one-and-one, and then Keith Gatlin stole the inbounds pass and was fouled. After Gatlin converted both of his free throws, the Terps suddenly had a 5-point lead and victory in hand.

"I thought the stall would be good for us because our players were tired," Navy coach Paul Evans said. "I thought we played well in the first 30 minutes, then I thought we maybe ran out of gas. Basically, they wore us down."

"I'd like to get to the Final Four before I die, but if it don't happen, so be it," Driessel said. When asked if it could happen this year, Maryland's jovial coach quipped, "Yeah, I could kick off anytime."

NAVY MIDSHIPMEN

	MIN	FGM-A	FTM-A	OFF	REB	AST	PF	PTS
Cliff Rees	27	3-6	0-0	-	1	3	2	6

	MIN	FGM-A	FTM-A	OFF	REB	AST	PF	PTS
Tony Wells	2	0-0	0-0	-	1	0	0	0
Kylor Whitaker	40	5-10	0-0	-	1	5	2	10
Doug Wojcik	40	0-1	0-0	-	2	7	4	0
David Robinson	38	11-18	0-3	-	8	0	2	22
	MIN	FGM-A	FTM-A	OFF	REB	AST	PF	PTS
Vernon Butler	40	4-8	4-5	-	8	3	1	12
Carl Liebert	13	3-4	3-4	-	2	0	1	9
TOTALS		FGM-A	FTM-A	OFF	REB	AST	PF	PTS
		26-47	7-12	-	23	18	12	59

MARYLAND TERRAPINS

	MIN	FGM-A	FTM-A	OFF	REB	AST	PF	PTS
Jeff Adkins	37	5-12	3-3	-	2	4	0	13
Jeff Baxter	1	0-0	0-0	-	0	0	0	0
Len Bias	40	7-11	6-9	-	8	1	3	20
Adrian Branch	29	5-13	1-1	-	2	1	4	11
Derrick Lewis	16	1-2	0-0	-	7	0	3	2
	MIN	FGM-A	FTM-A	OFF	REB	AST	PF	PTS
Thomas Jones	22	3-4	0-0	-	1	0	3	6
Keith Gatlin	40	4-8	2-2	-	1	12	1	10
Terry Long	15	1-1	0-0	-	2	0	2	2
TOTALS		FGM-A	FTM-A	OFF	REB	AST	PF	PTS
		26-51	12-15	-	23	18	16	64

Midwest Region

March 16
Tulsa, OK
1. Oklahoma 75
9. Illinois State 69

Being close to perfect just wasn't good enough for Wayman Tisdale. The Oklahoma All-American, who made 14 of 16 shots and scored 29 points, said his "performance could've been a lot better."

As a team, the 4th-ranked Sooners sank 66 percent of their shots and dominated the glass but still had trouble subduing the pesky Redbirds. Three times Oklahoma built double-digit leads only to see scrappy Illinois State pull close. First, the Sooners raced to an early 18-7 advantage before settling for a 4-point halftime lead. In the second half, the Big 8 champs were up by 10 before the Redbirds pulled within 57-54 with 7:30 remaining. Tisdale fueled a run that swelled the margin to 11 and Oklahoma coasted to victory.

"I would have liked them to roll over," Sooners coach Billy Tubbs said of his opponent. "We made the big plays and at times it looked like we were going to tuck it away."

Waiting for Oklahoma in the Sweet 16 was a Louisiana Tech team that the Sooners had already defeated earlier in the season, even though Tisdale endured the worst shooting game of his career at 3-for-16. Still, Tubbs didn't seem concerned about his superstar's offense or his run-and-gun team's defense. "We want to be the worst defensive team ever to win the NCAA," he said. "Nobody can hold the ball against us."

ILLINOIS STATE REDBIRDS

	MIN	FGM-A	FTM-A	OFF	REB	AST	PF	PTS
William Anderson	3	0-0	0-0	1	1	1	1	0
Matt Taphorn	11	1-2	0-0	0	1	2	0	2
Derrick Sanders	18	2-5	0-0	2	3	0	2	4
Lou Stefanovic	40	10-19	1-1	0	4	3	3	21
Michael McKenny	38	5-6	0-0	2	5	3	3	10
	MIN	FGM-A	FTM-A	OFF	REB	AST	PF	PTS
Tony Holifield	3	0-0	0-0	0	0	0	0	0
Bill Braksick	27	3-7	1-2	1	3	2	4	7
Rickie Johnson	32	6-10	2-3	0	2	4	2	14
Brad Duncan	28	5-12	1-1	0	1	0	1	11
TOTALS		FGM-A	FTM-A	OFF	REB	AST	PF	PTS
		32-61	5-7	6	20	15	16	69

OKLAHOMA SOONERS

	MIN	FGM-A	FTM-A	OFF	REB	AST	PF	PTS
Shawn Clark	10	2-4	0-0	0	0	1	1	4
Wayman Tisdale	40	14-16	1-4	1	8	0	3	29
Tim McCalister	40	6-12	0-1	0	2	7	2	12
Darryl Kennedy	37	7-10	2-2	2	8	7	2	16
Anthony Bowie	40	5-9	2-2	1	5	7	3	12
	MIN	FGM-A	FTM-A	OFF	REB	AST	PF	PTS
David Johnson	3	0-0	0-0	0	0	0	2	0
Linwood Davis	30	1-2	0-2	1	4	2	1	2
TOTALS		FGM-A	FTM-A	OFF	REB	AST	PF	PTS
		35-53	5-11	5	27	24	14	75

5. Louisiana Tech 79
4. Ohio State 67

The real Mailman finally made his rounds at the NCAA tournament. After an off game in the opening round in which he scored just 9 points, Karl Malone frolicked in the paint against Ohio State, destroying the Buckeyes with 27 points while pulling down 14 rebounds.

"Physically, Malone is as strong as any player we've played against this year," Ohio State coach Eldon Miller noted. "They're going to be a force to contend with down the road. They have an outstanding front line."

Another key part of that Tech front line, begoggled center Willie Simmons, also was a force with his intimidating defense and precise hook shots. Simmons and Malone led the Bulldogs to a 37-28 halftime lead before Malone salted the game away by scoring nine straight points after intermission as the "Dunkin Dawgs" stormed to a 46-30 advantage. Tech's margin grew to as much as 19 points, prompting their vocal supporters in Tulsa to follow up their "Big East, Big Deal" chant from the Pitt game with shouts of "Big Ten, Big Deal".

The Buckeyes, who relied all season on a talented but tiny trio of guards, figured to have a handful with the brawny Bulldogs. When Tech snapped awake after a slow start (Malone missed his first six shots) and built a sizable lead, Ohio State's hopes of controlling the tempo, and the game, were shattered.

OHIO STATE BUCKEYES								
	MIN	FGM-A	FTM-A	OFF	REB	AST	PF	PTS
John Anderson	3	0-0	0-0	-	0	0	0	0
Scott Anderson	1	0-0	0-0	-	1	0	0	0
Troy Taylor	35	9-18	0-1	-	3	7	4	18
Joe Concheck	30	2-6	0-0	-	6	2	3	4
Brad Sellers	30	3-8	0-0	-	6	0	5	6
	MIN	FGM-A	FTM-A	OFF	REB	AST	PF	PTS
Ronnie Stokes	39	3-9	5-6	-	3	5	4	11
Clarence McGee	1	0-0	0-0	-	1	0	0	0
Jim Honingford	1	0-0	0-0	-	0	0	1	0
Dennis Hopson	39	9-17	2-3	-	9	1	5	20
David Jones	21	4-6	0-0	-	2	1	0	8
TOTALS		FGM-A	FTM-A	OFF	REB	AST	PF	PTS
		30-64	7-10	-	31	16	22	67

LOUISIANA TECH BULLDOGS								
	MIN	FGM-A	FTM-A	OFF	REB	AST	PF	PTS
Roderick Hannibal	1	0-0	0-0	-	0	0	0	0
Keith Troutman	1	0-0	0-0	-	0	0	0	0

	MIN	FGM-A	FTM-A	OFF	REB	AST	PF	PTS
Willie Simmons	28	5-12	0-0	-	6	0	2	10
Wayne Smith	37	4-6	3-4	-	6	11	2	11
Adam Frank	19	3-5	3-3	-	2	4	1	9
	MIN	FGM-A	FTM-A	OFF	REB	AST	PF	PTS
Karl Malone	30	11-22	5-10	-	14	3	4	27
Willie Bland	25	3-5	2-4	-	4	1	0	8
Darryl Emerson	1	0-0	0-0	-	0	0	0	0
Kelvin Lewis	2	1-1	0-1	-	0	0	0	2
David Jordan	1	0-0	0-0	-	0	0	0	0
Alan Davis	21	3-3	0-0	-	0	1	5	6
Robert Godbolt	34	3-7	0-0	-	6	2	1	6
TOTALS		FGM-A	FTM-A	OFF	REB	AST	PF	PTS
		33-61	13-22	-	38	22	15	79

March 17
Houston, TX
11. Boston College 74
3. Duke 73

Duke's Mike Krzyzewski would routinely have Gary Williams' number when the latter coached at Maryland. But in their first meeting, it would be Williams who would get to savor a major victory over his soon-to-be rival.

In the early going, though, it looked like it would be an easy romp to the Sweet 16 for the 10th-ranked Blue Devils as they streaked to an 11-point lead. Duke stayed on top into the second half, when the Eagles finally got on track and rallied from a 49-41 deficit to take the lead for good at 59-57 with just under 11 minutes to play.

"In the first half, I was concerned. I thought maybe we had concluded a good season when they had an 11-point lead," Williams said. "But when we cut it to five points (at halftime), I felt we had a shot."

Boston College did indeed have a shot because Michael Adams and Roger McCready were hitting theirs. The duo combined for 39 points, many of them against what McCready called Duke's "soft" front line, while Blue Devils star Johnny Dawkins repeatedly tossed up bricks, missing 15 of his 21 attempts. "We didn't attack their 1-3-1 well at all," Coach K lamented. "We were trying to attack the zone, but we missed the shots."

Duke also missed super sixth man David Henderson for much of the game. Henderson, who blazed Pepperdine for 22 points in the opening round, scored just 2 against B.C. in limited action after the Eagles' Mark Schmidt fell onto his ankle. In addition, Mark Alarie, the Blue Devils' second leading scorer during the season, was still recovering from a recent hip pointer and was largely ineffective before fouling out.

Nevertheless, Duke was in position to pull out the victory despite trailing by 5 with 1:07 left when Dawkins converted a 3-point play with 29 seconds to go. However, the visibly tired Dawkins missed twice on the front end of 1-and-1's and the Blue Devils saw a trip to Dallas slip agonizingly through their fingers.

BOSTON COLLEGE EAGLES

	MIN	FGM-A	FTM-A	OFF	REB	AST	PF	PTS
Michael Adams	34	9-15	1-2	-	4	4	4	19
Skip Berry	12	2-6	0-0	-	4	0	1	4
Dominic Pressley	25	3-7	1-2	-	6	2	3	7
Stu Primus	25	3-6	2-2	-	3	3	3	8
Terrence Talley	21	0-0	2-3	-	2	0	4	2
	MIN	FGM-A	FTM-A	OFF	REB	AST	PF	PTS
Tyrone Scott	15	2-2	2-4	-	4	0	4	6
Mark Schmidt	11	0-1	0-0	-	1	2	3	0
Roger McCready	34	6-13	8-10	-	7	1	1	20
Troy Bowers	14	3-4	2-2	-	2	0	3	8
Trevor Gordon	9	0-0	0-2	-	0	0	2	0
TOTALS		FGM-A	FTM-A	OFF	REB	AST	PF	PTS
		28-54	18-27	-	33	12	28	74

DUKE BLUE DEVILS

	MIN	FGM-A	FTM-A	OFF	REB	AST	PF	PTS
Mark Alarie	30	5-12	2-2	-	6	1	5	12
Tommy Amaker	36	5-13	9-10	-	1	5	2	19
Weldon Williams	4	1-2	0-0	-	0	0	0	2
Kevin Strickland	2	0-0	0-0	-	1	0	1	0
Dan Meagher	34	1-3	1-3	-	7	4	4	3
	MIN	FGM-A	FTM-A	OFF	REB	AST	PF	PTS
Jay Bilas	37	4-7	7-10	-	13	4	3	15
Billy King	6	0-0	2-4	-	2	0	3	2
Johnny Dawkins	40	6-21	6-8	-	10	5	2	18
David Henderson	11	1-4	0-0	-	2	0	1	2
TOTALS		FGM-A	FTM-A	OFF	REB	AST	PF	PTS
		23-62	27-37	-	42	19	21	73

2. Memphis State 67
7. Alabama-Birmingham 66 (OT)

The "Battle of Memphis" would not soon be forgotten in the South. It was settled when one of the littlest combatants got off the final shot.

Andre Turner sank a 17-footer with six seconds left in overtime and then Vincent Askew blocked a desperation heave to deny UAB coach Gene Bartow, who once coached the Tigers and had several Memphis-area players on his team, a satisfying upset win.

"We played as good as we could play," said Bartow, who had guided Memphis State to the national championship game 12 years earlier. "We felt this would be a special game and I think the people who saw it would say it was a special game."

There might have been no need for Turner to rescue the Tigers if not for another maddening performance from star forward Keith Lee, who scored 28 points but was plagued for the second straight game by foul trouble before finally fouling out in overtime. Still, the All-American came through with a free throw with 20 seconds left in regulation to force OT.

Memphis State jumped to an early 8-point lead before UAB recovered to go ahead 32-27 at halftime with the help of a controversial basket. Archie Johnson was credited with two points when his dunk attempt rattled on the rim and popped back out of the hoop. The officials ruled the ball had gone far enough through the rim to count. A basket by Anthony Gordon (who had 14 points and 15 rebounds) with 39 seconds left in OT loomed even larger, as it gave the Blazers a 66-65 lead, but it only served to set the stage for Turner's "relaxing jump shot", as Tigers' coach Dana Kirk called it, that sent the Metro Conference champs on to Dallas.

ALABAMA-BIRMINGHAM BLAZERS								
	MIN	FGM-A	FTM-A	OFF	REB	AST	PF	PTS
Murry Bartow	3	0-0	0-0	0	0	0	0	0
James Ponder	44	5-13	8-9	1	4	1	2	18
Michael Charles	40	3-4	3-4	1	3	4	2	9
Eddie Collins	7	0-1	0-0	0	0	0	1	0
Tracy Foster	2	0-0	0-0	0	0	0	0	0
	MIN	FGM-A	FTM-A	OFF	REB	AST	PF	PTS
Steve Mitchell	41	6-15	1-2	0	2	1	3	13
Archie Johnson	13	2-3	0-0	3	4	0	2	4
Marvin Johnson	5	0-0	1-2	0	1	0	0	1
Anthony Gordon	41	6-13	2-2	10	15	1	2	14
Jerome Mincy	29	0-8	7-11	5	9	0	4	7
TOTALS		FGM-A	FTM-A	OFF	REB	AST	PF	PTS
		22-57	22-30	20	38	7	16	66

MEMPHIS STATE TIGERS							
	MIN	FGM-A	FTM-A	OFF	REB	AST	PF	PTS
Vincent Askew	41	1-3	0-0	0	5	7	3	2
William Bedford	37	3-12	0-1	3	6	0	3	6
Willie Becton	12	0-0	0-0	0	0	0	3	0
Andre Turner	45	11-17	1-2	0	0	8	4	23
John Wilfong	6	0-1	0-0	1	1	1	1	0
	MIN	FGM-A	FTM-A	OFF	REB	AST	PF	PTS
Baskerville Holmes	39	2-7	4-4	2	8	2	3	8
Dwight Boyd	9	0-2	0-0	2	3	0	2	0
Keith Lee	36	12-17	4-6	4	6	0	5	28
TOTALS		FGM-A	FTM-A	OFF	REB	AST	PF	PTS
		29-59	9-13	12	29	18	24	67

Regional Semifinals – Sweet 16

East Region

March 21

Providence, RI

1. Georgetown 65

4. Loyola (IL) 53

It was a classic David vs. Goliath matchup, and David was chirping like he didn't even need his slingshot in order to slay the giant.

"We are coming here with the feeling that we can beat Georgetown," Alfredrick Hughes said, while Andre Battle stated, "Georgetown likes to intimidate people, but we are pretty aggressive ourselves. We're city kids and we don't take any slack from anybody."

On the surface, at least, it seemed like the Ramblers had legitimate reasons to feel so confident. After all, Loyola had the longest winning streak in the nation at 19 games. In addition, three of their starters played on a high school team that nearly toppled a squad led by Hoyas great Patrick Ewing. And for the game's first 20 minutes, the Ramblers backed up their words, taking a 28-26 lead into the locker room at halftime as the sluggish top-ranked Hoyas committed 11 turnovers. Adding to Loyola's encouragement was the fact it led despite having Hughes, the fifth-leading scorer in NCAA history, on the bench for the last 10 minutes of the half after he was whistled for his third foul.

The Hoyas, however, did not win the 1984 championship and dominate the '84-'85 season by panicking. The 7-foot-1 Ewing exerted himself against the much smaller Ramblers (their tallest player was 6-9), scoring 14 of his game-high 21 points in the second half as he played with more fire because "I'm not ready to go home. I'm going to play as hard as I can to bring home the gold."

While Ewing rose to the occasion, Hughes disappeared. Loyola's scoring machine was broken and ended his college career with a 4-for-13 nightmare, thanks in large part to the blanket defense of Georgetown's Bill Martin. Hughes, who finished with 8 points, saw his streak of 95 straight games in double figures end. "This is my last year and it was an unfortunate way to end it," Hughes said. "That wasn't our game."

For a while it wasn't a typical Hoya game, either. But the Ramblers learned what numerous earlier victims had discovered – even when Georgetown wasn't at its best, it was still real good.

GEORGETOWN HOYAS

	MIN	FGM-A	FTM-A	OFF	REB	AST	PF	PTS
Ralph Dalton	9	1-1	1-2	2	4	0	0	3
Reggie Williams	24	2-7	4-4	2	5	1	3	8
David Wingate	34	7-14	0-1	2	3	1	0	14
Bill Martin	37	4-7	0-3	1	3	1	2	8
Perry McDonald	12	0-0	1-2	0	2	0	0	1
	MIN	FGM-A	FTM-A	OFF	REB	AST	PF	PTS
Ralph Highsmith	1	0-0	0-0	0	0	0	0	0
Tyrone Lockhart	1	0-0	0-0	0	0	0	0	0
Patrick Ewing	36	9-15	3-4	5	14	2	1	21
Horace Broadnax	11	0-2	2-2	0	1	0	1	2
Michael Jackson	35	3-8	2-3	3	7	12	2	8
TOTALS		FGM-A	FTM-A	OFF	REB	AST	PF	PTS
		26-54	13-21	15	39	17	9	65

LOYOLA (IL) RAMBLERS

	MIN	FGM-A	FTM-A	OFF	REB	AST	PF	PTS
Ivan Young	17	1-5	0-0	1	3	0	0	2
Andre Battle	39	5-13	0-0	1	3	0	4	10
Mike Cenar	7	1-2	0-0	0	0	0	2	2
Greg Williams	27	2-4	0-0	1	3	3	5	4
Dave Klusendorf	1	0-1	0-0	0	0	0	0	0
	MIN	FGM-A	FTM-A	OFF	REB	AST	PF	PTS
Nate Brooks	1	0-0	0-0	0	0	0	1	0
Carl Golston	39	3-12	0-0	1	3	7	2	6
Andre Moore	39	8-13	3-3	5	8	1	3	19
Alfredrick Hughes	29	4-13	0-1	1	5	0	3	8
Bobby Clark	1	1-2	0-0	1	2	0	0	2
TOTALS		FGM-A	FTM-A	OFF	REB	AST	PF	PTS
		25-65	3-4	11	27	11	20	53

2. Georgia Tech 61
3. Illinois 53

Practice didn't quite make Mark Price perfect, but it did enough to make him unstoppable on this night.

"I went to Providence College on Wednesday and practiced shooting for 30 minutes," Georgia Tech's star guard said. "I got my shot back. It sure helped today."

Price, who had made only 11 of his 27 field goal attempts in the first two rounds, drained 9 of 12 against Illinois for a team-high 20 points as the Yellow Jackets blitzed the Illini after intermission following a dead-even first half. For the game, Tech sank 56 percent of its attempts against an Illinois squad that was second in the nation in field goal defense for the season at 41.5 percent.

"It was hard to cover Price," Illini coach Lou Henson said. "He was the key to the game. He hurt us early. He hurt us all game."

Another key to game was the disappearing act of two of Henson's main players. Forward Efrem Winters was dominated by Tech's twin towers of John Salley and Yvon Joseph and failed to score in the game's last 34 minutes. Meanwhile, point guard Bruce Douglas finished with a brutal stat line: 1-of-6 shooting, one assist and nine turnovers.

Price's long-range bombs and some easy baskets inside for Salley and Joseph lifted the Jackets to a 52-37 lead with seven minutes remaining. Illinois' reliable Doug Altenberger then snapped into action, putting on an impressive shooting display as he single-handedly rallied the Illini within 55-51 before fouling out with 1:25 left. Sixth-ranked Tech then salted the game away from the foul line, earning a shot at No. 1 Georgetown.

"Altenberger put on a show," Georgia Tech coach Bobby Cremins raved. "I always thought Price was the greatest shooter in college basketball, but Altenberger made me consider him." Nevertheless, after shredding the nation's No. 2 defense, it would be Price who would get to test his marksmanship against the Hoyas' top-ranked stoppers.

GEORGIA TECH YELLOW JACKETS								
	MIN	FGM-A	FTM-A	OFF	REB	AST	PF	PTS
Scott Petway	28	0-2	2-2	1	2	2	2	2
Mark Price	38	9-12	2-3	0	2	2	0	20
Bruce Dalrymple	36	3-4	2-4	0	4	3	2	8
John Salley	36	5-12	4-5	1	4	3	3	14
Duane Ferrell	16	1-3	1-2	1	1	2	0	3
	MIN	FGM-A	FTM-A	OFF	REB	AST	PF	PTS
Antoine Ford	7	0-0	0-0	0	1	0	1	0
John Martinson	2	0-0	0-0	0	0	0	0	0
Jack Mansell	2	0-0	0-0	0	0	0	0	0

	MIN	FGM-A	FTM-A	OFF	REB	AST	PF	PTS
Yvon Joseph	35	4-6	6-8	1	3	1	4	14
TOTALS		FGM-A	FTM-A	OFF	REB	AST	PF	PTS
		22-39	17-24	4	17	13	12	61

ILLINOIS FIGHTING ILLINI

	MIN	FGM-A	FTM-A	OFF	REB	AST	PF	PTS
Doug Altenberger	38	11-17	2-3	1	3	1	5	24
Ken Norman	38	3-3	3-3	1	7	7	3	9
Anthony Welch	37	5-10	0-0	2	5	2	0	10
Efrem Winters	36	2-5	0-2	2	4	1	3	4
Tony Wysinger	12	0-4	0-0	0	1	2	3	0
	MIN	FGM-A	FTM-A	OFF	REB	AST	PF	PTS
Bruce Douglas	33	1-6	2-2	1	2	1	2	4
Scott Meents	6	1-2	0-0	0	0	1	4	2
TOTALS		FGM-A	FTM-A	OFF	REB	AST	PF	PTS
		23-47	7-10	7	22	15	20	53

West Region

March 22

Denver, CO

1. St. John's 86

12. Kentucky 70

St. John's All-American Chris Mullin was left unguarded often enough to score 30 points, but he managed to get close enough to one important Kentucky player in order to (unintentionally) do some serious damage.

With the Wildcats leading 20-13 and looking like a real threat to advance to the regional finals as a No. 12 seed, Mullin poked Kentucky's Kenny Walker in the eye with his finger, causing the Wildcat high-flyer to leave the game temporarily and sucking the life out of the Cinderella Cats.

"Chris said his finger felt like it went all the way through Kenny's eye. You could hear it, like squish. Ugly," the Redmen's Willie Glass observed. Walker heroically would return and finish with 23 points despite his eye being almost swollen shut. Meanwhile, led by Glass, St. John's controlled the glass, using numerous second-chance baskets to turn a 39-38 halftime edge into a comfortable victory margin. Glass' three put-backs in the second half were especially damaging to Kentucky.

"They beat us badly in the second half on the offensive boards," said Joe B. Hall, who coached his final game at Kentucky. "On all but four possessions they got second shots, and we couldn't contend with that. That was our biggest breakdown."

An even bigger breakdown might have occurred in Kentucky's defense, as the sharp-eyed Mullin was given free rein to bomb away. Mullin later acknowledged that he was "pretty wide open all night. They were probably the easiest shots I got all year. It was like being out of jail for a night."

Hall wasted no time addressing the rumors of his retirement by saying on his postgame radio show that he was indeed stepping down after 13 years at the Kentucky helm. "I looked around and decided I didn't want to be an old coach," he said.

ST. JOHN'S REDMEN								
	MIN	FGM-A	FTM-A	OFF	REB	AST	PF	PTS
Bill Wennington	24	4-7	2-2	-	3	2	4	10
Ron Stewart	16	1-1	0-0	-	2	0	1	2
Walter Berry	36	7-13	8-11	-	12	2	4	22
Mike Moses	21	0-3	0-0	-	0	1	2	0
Chris Mullin	40	11-23	8-10	-	5	7	0	30
	MIN	FGM-A	FTM-A	OFF	REB	AST	PF	PTS
Mark Jackson	19	3-4	6-8	-	2	4	2	12
Shelton Jones	6	0-0	0-0	-	0	0	0	0
Willie Glass	38	4-5	2-2	-	9	3	1	10
TOTALS		FGM-A	FTM-A	OFF	REB	AST	PF	PTS
		30-56	26-33	-	33	19	14	86

KENTUCKY WILDCATS								
	MIN	FGM-A	FTM-A	OFF	REB	AST	PF	PTS
Paul Andrews	2	0-0	0-0	-	0	0	0	0
Todd Ziegler	1	0-0	0-0	-	0	0	0	0
Bret Bearup	19	1-3	0-0	-	3	2	5	2
Kenny Walker	36	10-14	3-3	-	8	4	5	23
Roger Harden	28	6-10	1-1	-	2	7	3	13
	MIN	FGM-A	FTM-A	OFF	REB	AST	PF	PTS
Winston Bennett	24	2-2	2-2	-	3	0	5	6
Ed Davender	25	5-10	1-2	-	3	3	2	11
Richard Madison	29	2-9	1-3	-	4	1	1	5
Troy McKinley	16	4-6	0-0	-	2	1	1	8
James Blackmon	13	0-4	0-0	-	1	1	1	0
Leroy Byrd	1	0-0	0-0	-	0	0	0	0
Cedric Jenkins	3	1-1	0-0	-	1	0	0	2
Robert Lock	3	0-0	0-0	-	0	0	1	0
TOTALS		FGM-A	FTM-A	OFF	REB	AST	PF	PTS
		31-59	8-11	-	27	19	24	70

3. North Carolina State 61
7. Alabama 55

Spud Webb would one day be known for his amazing dunking skills, but on this night it was his defense that had people talking. The 5-foot-6 guard's hustle helped force a turnover when Alabama seemed on the verge of a game-tying basket in the last minute to cap a frustrating final nine minutes for the underdog Crimson Tide.

After missing the front end of a one-and-one, Webb stepped in front of Alabama's Terry Coner on a fastbreak, causing Coner to misfire on his pass to a wide-open Jim Farmer. N.C. State's Bennie Bolton corralled the loose ball, was fouled and made both free throws to up the Pack's lead to 57-53 with 33 seconds left, and the Tide never got any closer.

"What happened was Spud ran under him (Coner)," Farmer said. "When he couldn't get a clear pass, he kind of tried to swat the ball to me. The ball just bounced the wrong way. That happens sometimes."

It's what didn't happen at the free throw line that killed Alabama. The Tide made only 9 of 18 attempts for the game, including just 4 of 9 during those crucial final nine minutes when Bama saw a 4-point lead slip away. "Our free throw shooting was not real good. And if you look at that, it could have been the difference in the game," Tide coach Wimp Sanderson noted.

Two Wolfpack subs also made a big difference. Bolton (11 points) and Terry Gannon (8) provided much-needed long-range scoring after Alabama had effectively smothered N.C. State's big men. "Gannon and Bolton kept us in it," Pack coach Jim Valvano said. "At one point, Bolton hit four straight and, in the second half, Gannon hit three straight."

Mighty St. John's now stood between North Carolina State and a second Final Four visit in three years, but fans and members of the media were perhaps expecting to be more entertained by the verbal bantering of Valvano and his *paisan*, Redmen coach Lou Carnesecca. "I can honestly say that if we lose, I will be terribly disappointed," Valvano said. "But there would be a certain happiness for Looie, too."

NORTH CAROLINA STATE WOLFPACK							
	MIN	FGM-A	FTM-A	OFF REB	AST	PF	PTS
Russell Pierre	29	2-4	4-5	- 6	0	2	8
John Thompson	1	0-0	0-0	- 0	0	0	0
Lorenzo Charles	35	5-11	4-6	- 6	3	0	14
Spud Webb	38	5-12	4-6	- 4	5	4	14
Cozell McQueen	25	2-5	0-0	- 4	0	5	4
	MIN	FGM-A	FTM-A	OFF REB	AST	PF	PTS
Bennie Bolton	30	4-8	3-4	- 1	1	2	11
Terry Gannon	14	4-4	0-0	- 0	2	1	8

	MIN	FGM-A	FTM-A	OFF	REB	AST	PF	PTS
Nate McMillan	22	0-2	2-6	-	0	0	2	2
Ernie Myers	6	0-1	0-0	-	0	0	2	0
TOTALS		FGM-A	FTM-A	OFF	REB	AST	PF	PTS
		22-47	17-27	-	26	15	19	61

ALABAMA CRIMSON TIDE

	MIN	FGM-A	FTM-A	OFF	REB	AST	PF	PTS
Darrell Neal	9	0-2	0-0	-	2	0	0	0
Terry Coner	33	6-10	6-10	-	4	4	4	18
Jim Farmer	25	2-4	0-0	-	1	3	3	4
Mark Farmer	1	0-0	0-0	-	0	0	0	0
Derrick McKey	32	3-8	0-0	-	4	1	5	6
	MIN	FGM-A	FTM-A	OFF	REB	AST	PF	PTS
Buck Johnson	38	7-11	2-5	-	14	2	5	16
Mark Gottfried	23	1-6	0-0	-	0	2	2	2
Bobby Lee Hurt	39	4-9	1-3	-	5	0	2	9
TOTALS		FGM-A	FTM-A	OFF	REB	AST	PF	PTS
		23-50	9-18	-	30	12	21	55

Southeast Region

March 22
Birmingham, AL
8. Villanova 46
4. Maryland 43

When Maryland met Villanova two months earlier, the Terrapins eked out a close win in a high-scoring affair. The rematch would be just as close, but without nearly as much offense, especially from one key player.

Len Bias, who had tormented the Wildcats with a career-high 30 points in their 77-74 shootout on Jan. 27 in College Park, Md., was held to 8 points on 4-of-13 shooting this time, thanks in large part to the defensive effort of Ed Pinckney. "Pinckney just guarded me well," said Bias, whose total was his lowest of the season and ended his string of 53 straight double-digit scoring games. "He got in my way in the lane. He didn't do that much in the first game."

"Len was getting frustrated," Villanova's Harold Pressley said. "He was firing bad shots. And Eddie made him think. Eddie got to him early, and that was important."

No less important was Pinckney's offensive contribution. After the teams slogged through a first half that ended with the Terrapins clinging to a 20-19 lead, the Wildcats finally came to life early in the second period by ripping off an 11-0 run that was fueled by Pinckney's seven points. The Terps, meanwhile, misfired on their first eight shots of the half but still managed to claw within 43-40 with two minutes left.

Villanova coach Rollie Massimino was a master of delay tactics and his 'Cats milked a minute off the clock before being sent to the foul line and ultimately icing the victory.

"We had three days to prepare for that game," Villanova's Gary McLain said of the first meeting. "We had all week to prepare for this one. You figure we should win if we have that much time."

For the Wildcats' three senior stars – Pinckney, McLain and Dwayne McClain – it would be their third regional final in four years and their last shot at the elusive Final Four. "We'll go as far as we take ourselves," a confident Pinckney said. "The only team that can beat us is ourselves."

VILLANOVA WILDCATS

	MIN	FGM-A	FTM-A	OFF	REB	AST	PF	PTS
Ed Pinckney	36	5-7	6-7	-	13	1	4	16
Mark Plansky	13	2-3	0-0	-	4	2	0	4
Harold Pressley	35	3-12	1-4	-	10	1	2	7
Dwight Wilbur	25	1-5	2-2	-	4	3	0	4
Dwayne McClain	40	5-9	2-2	-	4	2	3	12
	MIN	FGM-A	FTM-A	OFF	REB	AST	PF	PTS
Chuck Everson	4	0-0	0-0	-	0	0	0	0
Harold Jensen	11	0-5	0-1	-	0	1	1	0
Gary McLain	36	1-5	1-2	-	2	1	0	3
TOTALS		FGM-A	FTM-A	OFF	REB	AST	PF	PTS
		17-46	12-18	-	37	11	10	46

MARYLAND TERRAPINS

	MIN	FGM-A	FTM-A	OFF	REB	AST	PF	PTS
Jeff Adkins	29	2-7	0-0	-	4	4	2	4
Jeff Baxter	10	2-2	0-0	-	0	0	2	4
Len Bias	40	4-13	0-0	-	5	1	4	8
Adrian Branch	39	9-19	3-5	-	5	2	3	21
Derrick Lewis	24	0-2	0-0	-	5	0	4	0
	MIN	FGM-A	FTM-A	OFF	REB	AST	PF	PTS
Thomas Jones	12	0-2	0-0	-	2	1	3	0
Keith Gatlin	30	2-7	0-0	-	4	2	1	4
Terry Long	16	0-1	2-2	-	4	0	1	2
TOTALS		FGM-A	FTM-A	OFF	REB	AST	PF	PTS
		19-53	5-7	-	29	10	20	43

2. North Carolina 62
11. Auburn 56

A slow start and a Carolina Blue mountain range proved too much for Cinderella Auburn to overcome. North Carolina amassed a 15-point first-half lead and then held on in the face of a ferocious Tigers rally thanks to its decided size advantage.

With four players each at least 6-feet-10 in height, the Tar Heels converted several easy layups as they raced to a 19-5 lead just 6:30 into the game. "They played extremely well early in the ballgame," said Auburn coach Sonny Smith, whose team had won the SEC championship two weeks earlier on the same floor. "I think the game was won by Carolina in the first five minutes."

Complicating matters for Smith was the unusually cold shooting of star forward Chuck Person. "The Rifleman", who misfired on 17 of his 25 shot attempts, said, "I guess I was pressing too much. I wanted to go out and score six points for every shot."

Person was at the center of a controversial play that might have decided the game. After the Tigers had pecked away at Carolina's lead and finally drew within 58-56 with 18 seconds remaining, Person grabbed a rebound and fell to the floor with the ball. Traveling was called, eliciting a hail of boos from the partisan Birmingham crowd, but Person, for one, defended the ruling. "I wasn't pushed," he said. "I fell into somebody. It was my fault, it wasn't his. The referee made a great call."

The debatable traveling call never would have been a factor if not for Auburn's defensive adjustment, which saw the Tigers collapse on North Carolina's big men and cut off the short shot attempts. But that cleared the stage for Tar Heels guard Kenny Smith, who victimized Auburn's backcourt with a career-high 22 points. "I think our ability to contain, to a degree, their inside game was a key to our comeback," Sonny Smith noted. "But when you do that, you make Kenny Smith very effective."

The game's "third Smith", Heels coach Dean, earned his 31st career NCAA tournament victory, moving him into sole possession of second place, 16 behind John Wooden. But it would be Sonny who would draw the headlines four days later when he retracted his earlier decision to resign at the end of the season and instead announced that he would remain Auburn's coach.

AUBURN TIGERS

	MIN	FGM-A	FTM-A	OFF	REB	AST	PF	PTS
Chuck Person	39	8-25	0-0	-	12	3	4	16
Gerald White	37	2-5	0-0	-	1	2	4	4
Frank Ford	37	8-14	1-2	-	4	3	2	17
Carey Holland	22	2-2	4-8	-	1	0	2	8
Johnny Lynn	5	0-0	0-0	-	0	0	1	0
	MIN	FGM-A	FTM-A	OFF	REB	AST	PF	PTS
Darren Guest	5	0-0	0-0	-	1	0	0	0
Jeff Moore	17	2-3	0-0	-	2	1	3	4

	MIN	FGM-A	FTM-A	OFF	REB	AST	PF	PTS
Chris Morris	38	3-10	1-2	-	9	0	2	7
TOTALS		FGM-A	FTM-A	OFF	REB	AST	PF	PTS
		25-59	6-12	-	30	9	18	56

NORTH CAROLINA TAR HEELS

	MIN	FGM-A	FTM-A	OFF	REB	AST	PF	PTS
Buzz Peterson	29	0-5	0-0	-	2	2	2	0
Dave Popson	14	2-4	0-0	-	4	0	1	4
Brad Daugherty	39	5-8	0-2	-	8	3	2	10
Joe Wolf	35	4-6	2-2	-	7	3	3	10
Kenny Smith	38	9-12	4-5	-	3	6	1	22
	MIN	FGM-A	FTM-A	OFF	REB	AST	PF	PTS
Ranzino Smith	14	1-5	2-2	-	2	1	0	4
Warren Martin	26	4-8	4-5	-	5	1	3	12
Chris Hunter	5	0-1	0-2	-	1	0	0	0
TOTALS		FGM-A	FTM-A	OFF	REB	AST	PF	PTS
		25-49	12-18	-	32	16	12	62

Midwest Region

March 21

Dallas, TX

1. Oklahoma 86
5. Louisiana Tech 84 (OT)

With its best player not performing at his usual All-American level, top-seeded Oklahoma was pushed to the brink. But when the Sooners needed Wayman Tisdale the most he produced, bouncing in a 6-foot jumper with three seconds remaining to give fifth-ranked Oklahoma a heart-stopping overtime victory.

After Louisiana Tech had tied the game at 84 with 18 seconds to play, the Sooners patiently worked for a final shot but had trouble getting the ball to the triple-teamed Tisdale. The 6-foot-9 junior finally got it near the lane, turned and floated up a shot with his familiar soft left-handed touch.

"It seems like it took forever on the rim," said Tisdale of his game-winner, which bounced five times on the iron before going in. "I just wanted to turn and shoot it as soft as I could. I wasn't trying to run off as much time as I did." Bulldogs coach Andy Russo had a similar take, saying, "That shot hung on the rim for 10 minutes. But you have got to give him credit. He wanted the ball, he got it and he hit it."

The Sooners probably never should have needed a lucky bounce to subdue Tech, a team they had defeated by 12 points in December. After a slow start, the Big Eight champs used a 12-point run to take a 32-28 halftime lead and built their advantage to 10 in the second half. The Sooners got a boost when Tech's 6-10 expert shot-blocker, Willie Simmons, was called for his fourth foul with 16:16 to play. But

Oklahoma's sloppy ball-handling (17 turnovers) helped give the Bulldogs a chance to fight back, which they did behind their own frontcourt force, Karl Malone.

"The Mailman" was more than a match for Tisdale, scoring 20 points (many on long-range jumpers) and hauling in 16 rebounds while helping to put Tisdale in foul trouble. Tech turned the tables on the Sooners with an effective full-court press of their own that produced several easy baskets, but the final few minutes of regulation were a comedy of turnovers, missed shots and clanged free throws from both sides before Willie Bland scored on a put-back with 20 seconds to go to send the game into overtime.

"A lot of guys didn't have the point total they wanted, so they wanted to play five more minutes. I think Wayman was one of those," sarcastic Sooners coach Billy Tubbs said. Fortunately for Tubbs, Tisdale, who survived the final 14 minutes of action with four fouls, found his touch in the extra period. He scored 8 of his 23 points in overtime, but it was his final two that seemed to take forever that would be remembered for a long time.

LOUISIANA TECH BULLDOGS

	MIN	FGM-A	FTM-A	OFF	REB	AST	PF	PTS
Willie Simmons	24	3-11	4-4	2	2	1	4	10
Wayne Smith	42	2-11	2-2	2	5	8	1	6
Adam Frank	8	0-2	2-2	0	1	3	0	2
Karl Malone	45	9-19	2-4	6	16	3	4	20
Willie Bland	29	7-11	4-6	6	6	1	2	18
	MIN	FGM-A	FTM-A	OFF	REB	AST	PF	PTS
Alan Davis	40	9-15	0-0	2	6	8	3	18
Robert Godbolt	37	4-15	2-3	3	5	2	3	10
TOTALS		FGM-A	FTM-A	OFF	REB	AST	PF	PTS
		34-84	16-21	21	41	26	17	84

OKLAHOMA SOONERS

	MIN	FGM-A	FTM-A	OFF	REB	AST	PF	PTS
Chuck Watson	1	0-0	0-0	0	0	0	0	0
Shawn Clark	1	0-0	0-0	0	0	0	0	0
Wayman Tisdale	40	10-17	3-7	5	11	1	4	23
Tim McCalister	45	5-18	0-0	0	3	3	3	10
Darryl Kennedy	43	8-11	5-7	3	11	3	5	21
	MIN	FGM-A	FTM-A	OFF	REB	AST	PF	PTS
Anthony Bowie	45	8-11	0-1	2	10	7	1	16
David Johnson	31	4-5	2-3	1	4	3	5	10
Linwood Davis	19	2-5	2-2	1	1	1	2	6
TOTALS		FGM-A	FTM-A	OFF	REB	AST	PF	PTS
		37-67	12-20	12	40	18	20	86

2. Memphis State 59
11. Boston College 57

Playing the role of hero had quickly become old hat for Memphis State's Andre Turner. Four days after he made a 17-footer with five seconds left to sink Alabama-Birmingham, the diminutive guard again struck from 17 feet, this time at the buzzer, to give the Tigers another upset-averting victory.

"I'm never happy to have to take that last shot. I'd rather be up by 12," said the 5-foot-10 junior. Instead of celebrating with his teammates, Turner made a bee-line for the locker room. "I was trying not to jubilate all about the court," he explained.

"I'm going to put a sixth star on his five-star general status," Tigers coach Dana Kirk said of Turner, who was known as the "Little General". "Boston College was tough," he added. "They can get back into a game just about as fast as you can get into one."

In this instance, the scrappy Eagles came back from 12 down by scoring a dozen consecutive points to tie the game at 57 with 4:30 remaining. With under a minute to play, B.C. had possession and a chance at the final shot. But Roger McCready couldn't handle an inbounds pass and Vincent Askew alertly scooped up the ball for Memphis State before passing it to Turner, who calmly dribbled into open space before firing his game-winner.

"It's the toughest loss I've ever had," Eagles coach Gary Williams said. "But I'm proud that we came as far as we did." Williams' squad might have gone farther if not for Michael Adams' off night. The B.C. guard, whose own last-second shot against Texas Tech had given the Eagles a first-round win, was held to 12 points on 6-of-14 shooting.

Adams wasn't the only star who struggled. Memphis State All-American Keith Lee's dreadful tournament continued as he was once again plagued by foul trouble (three fouls in the game's first five minutes) and made only 3 of 12 shots for 8 points. However, 7-foot sophomore William Bedford more than picked up the slack in the paint with a career-high 23 points for the Tigers. Bedford keyed Memphis State's burst out of the halftime break, scoring three straight baskets as the Tigers turned a tie game into a 47-35 lead, but he missed the front end of a one-and-one with over 2 minutes to play. The Eagles got the rebound and held the ball until there were just 14 seconds on the clock, setting the stage for Askew's steal.

BOSTON COLLEGE EAGLES								
	MIN	FGM-A	FTM-A	OFF	REB	AST	PF	PTS
Michael Adams	-	6-14	0-0	-	2	4	2	12
Skip Barry	-	0-5	0-0	-	4	1	0	0
Dominic Pressley	-	1-2	0-0	-	1	1	0	2
Stu Primus	-	7-13	0-0	-	3	1	2	14
Terrence Talley	-	5-8	1-2	-	4	1	4	11

	MIN	FGM-A	FTM-A	OFF	REB	AST	PF	PTS
Tyrone Scott	-	0-0	0-0	-	0	0	0	0
Mark Schmidt	-	0-1	0-0	-	0	1	0	0
Roger McCready	-	2-7	5-6	-	3	0	1	9
Troy Bowers	-	0-2	0-0	-	2	0	3	0
Trevor Gordon	-	3-3	3-5	-	6	0	4	9
TOTALS		FGM-A	FTM-A	OFF	REB	AST	PF	PTS
		24-55	9-13	-	25	9	16	57

MEMPHIS STATE TIGERS

	MIN	FGM-A	FTM-A	OFF	REB	AST	PF	PTS
Vincent Askew	-	1-3	0-0	-	4	9	0	2
William Bedford	-	10-13	3-4	-	8	0	3	23
Willie Becton	-	4-10	0-0	-	5	0	2	8
Andre Turner	-	6-12	0-0	-	2	7	1	12
Baskerville Holmes	-	2-7	0-0	-	3	1	2	4
	MIN	FGM-A	FTM-A	OFF	REB	AST	PF	PTS
Dwight Boyd	-	1-1	0-1	-	0	0	0	2
Keith Lee	-	3-12	2-3	-	8	4	4	8
TOTALS		FGM-A	FTM-A	OFF	REB	AST	PF	PTS
		27-58	5-8	-	30	21	12	59

Regional Finals – Elite 8

East Region

March 23

Providence, RI

1. Georgetown 60

2. Georgia Tech 54

Just when the seemingly invincible Hoyas appeared ripe for the taking, they gave definitive proof that they were more than just one man, while Georgia Tech learned that it was more dependent on one star that it had probably imagined.

With All-American center Patrick Ewing on the bench for 12 minutes of the second half with foul trouble, Georgetown leaned on its unheralded role players to earn its 16th straight win and third Final Four berth in the last four years. The defending champs' trip to Lexington was looking unlikely when disaster seemed to strike with 18 minutes left. The Hoyas led by just one point when Ewing was whistled for his fourth foul after he had dominated the first half with 12 of his team-best 14 points. But instead of falling to pieces without their 7-foot leader, Georgetown showed the character of a champion by actually increasing its lead to 48-44 by the time Ewing returned with 5:30 remaining.

"I know the team had everything under control," Ewing said. "I had confidence in them." Added Hoya coach John Thompson: "Other people realize their responsibilities when Patrick is not in the game."

One of those "other people" was Ralph Dalton. Ewing's 6-foot-11 backup went shoulder-to-shoulder with Tech's twin towers, John Salley and Yvon Joseph, and gave the Hoyas 25 effective minutes after having played 28 minutes total in the team's first three tourney games. It was Dalton on the line with 14 seconds left and Georgetown up 2, and he calmly sank both ends of a one-and-one to seal the victory.

Another Hoya who stepped into the spotlight was forward Bill Martin. The always tenacious defender, in tandem with Dalton, held Joseph to 1-of-4 shooting and Salley to just 6 of his game-high 15 points during those crucial minutes when Ewing was sidelined. "Myself and Ralph tried to rally the guys so there wouldn't be an emotional letdown with Pat out of the game," Martin said. "We may have picked the intensity up a little, especially defensively."

The Yellow Jackets, on the other hand, had no one step up when their top player, Mark Price, was mired in one of his most miserable games ever. Two days after sinking 9 of 12 shots against Illinois' second-ranked field goal defense, the junior guard misfired on 13 of his 16 attempts against Georgetown's No. 1 defense.

"It's too bad Mark Price had a tough shooting day. We would not be here without Mark Price," Tech coach Bobby Cremins said. Thompson wasn't about to dish out any praise for Price's long day. "I don't think we did a good job on Price," he said. "He got our big people in foul trouble, so I don't think you can really say that we did a job on him."

If not for making 22 of their 24 free throws, the Yellow Jackets probably never would have made a game of it. Tech, which trailed 28-21, scrambled back to tie the score at 29 at halftime after Thompson went to a spread offense that only seemed to slow his team down and kill its momentum. The Hoyas' troubles persisted in the second half, but Georgetown's impressive depth ultimately carried the day. Horace Broadnax and Reggie Williams combined for 21 points, Dalton's put-back with 7:20 left gave the Hoyas the lead for good at 46-44 (after the Jackets had held a four-point edge) and then Ewing returned to help finally subdue Tech.

Thompson sounded weary after his team took a step that many had considered a foregone conclusion. "It's getting harder and harder," he said of going to the Final Four. "The championship is easier than getting to it."

GEORGETOWN HOYAS								
	MIN	FGM-A	FTM-A	OFF	REB	AST	PF	PTS
Ralph Dalton	25	1-2	4-4	2	6	0	4	6
Reggie Williams	33	4-6	4-4	4	5	2	3	12
David Wingate	34	3-8	1-2	1	1	1	3	7

	MIN	FGM-A	FTM-A	OFF	REB	AST	PF	PTS
Bill Martin	32	5-10	2-3	1	2	0	4	12
Grady Mateen	3	0-0	0-0	1	1	0	0	0
	MIN	FGM-A	FTM-A	OFF	REB	AST	PF	PTS
Perry McDonald	2	0-1	0-0	1	2	0	0	0
Patrick Ewing	25	5-9	4-9	2	4	1	4	14
Horace Broadnax	18	3-4	3-4	0	3	1	0	9
Michael Jackson	28	0-6	0-0	1	1	5	4	0
TOTALS		FGM-A	FTM-A	OFF	REB	AST	PF	PTS
		21-46	18-26	13	25	10	22	60

GEORGIA TECH YELLOW JACKETS

	MIN	FGM-A	FTM-A	OFF	REB	AST	PF	PTS
Scott Petway	24	1-2	0-0	0	0	4	3	2
Mark Price	40	3-16	7-8	1	1	1	1	13
Bruce Dalrymple	38	3-5	7-7	4	4	0	4	13
John Salley	29	5-8	5-5	1	5	2	5	15
Duane Ferrell	18	1-3	0-0	3	4	0	3	2
	MIN	FGM-A	FTM-A	OFF	REB	AST	PF	PTS
Antoine Ford	12	2-2	2-2	0	1	1	2	6
Jack Mansell	1	0-0	0-0	0	0	0	0	0
Yvon Joseph	38	1-4	1-2	2	4	2	4	3
TOTALS		FGM-A	FTM-A	OFF	REB	AST	PF	PTS
		16-40	22-24	11	19	10	22	54

Midwest Region

March 23
Dallas, TX
2. Memphis State 63
1. Oklahoma 61

Considering Memphis State and Oklahoma were coming off heart-stopping last-second victories, it was only appropriate that their meeting would come down to the wire. And it figured that the drama would once again center on the Tigers' Andre Turner, who had turned the NCAA tournament into his stage for a series of unforgettable one-man dramas.

Turner, who had already won two tourney games with clutch late-game shots, scored four points in the frantic final 33 seconds to help send Memphis State to its first Final Four since 1973. But the point guard almost got the goat horns when he missed the front end of a one-and-one with 8 seconds on the clock, giving Oklahoma one last chance. Turner was let off the hook, however, when Anthony Bowie's desperate 24-foot heave at the horn clanged off the back of the rim.

"I was real glad it didn't come down to where I had to make a last-second shot again," said a relieved Turner, who was masterful in producing 12 points to go along with his 12 assists as he wrapped up the regional most valuable player award.

Turner surprisingly outscored Oklahoma's prolific All-American forward, Wayman Tisdale. Two days after he had bounced in the winning hoop in overtime against Louisiana Tech, Tisdale found shots hard to come by against Memphis State's towering duo of William Bedford and Keith Lee and finished with only 11 points. The offensive woes extended to Tisdale's teammates, as the nation's highest scoring team was held 29 points below its season average.

"We're not going to get our heads down. We'll just have to come back next year and be better," Tisdale said. But there would be no next year for Tisdale in a Sooners uniform. The junior, who had been an All-American all three years at Oklahoma, decided to forego his senior season and enter the NBA draft, where he was selected second overall.

One of Tisdale's tormentors, Lee, continued to be plagued by foul trouble (it took him just 17 seconds to earn his first foul of the game). He managed to avoid fouling out but still was limited to 27 minutes on the floor. He made the most of that playing time, scoring a game-high 23 points and pulling down 11 rebounds. The Tigers' All-American scored a basket and sank four free throws in the game's final 1:30, but his contribution seemed to pale in comparison to Turner's. During one crucial stretch midway through the second half, after the Sooners' had cut their deficit to two, Turner twice fed Bedford perfect alley-oop passes before sinking two jumpers in the lane to restore the Tigers' lead to six.

A non-call involving Turner had Oklahoma coach Billy Tubbs steamed. Tubbs thought that Turner should have been called for a turnover instead of being sent to the foul line with eight seconds remaining. "Everybody in the place knew it was a turnover," Tubbs fumed. "You do what you can do but there are three guys (referees) who determine your future. You pray they have the guts to make the call."

Tubbs was even more annoyed by the pounding that Tisdale took in the lane. "How do you get it (the ball) to a guy who is full-nelsoned and pounded all night? He's the most abused player in America," Tubbs said.

Tisdale's decision to go pro meant he could be well compensated for his bruises, but it also put a sour cap on what had ultimately been a disappointing season for the Sooners. As for the Tigers, they got the distinction of being the party-crasher at a Final Four that had become a mini Big East tournament. "I want to wear the roses around my neck," Memphis State coach Dana Kirk said. "I think we've got a good basketball team and however far we go we deserve it."

MEMPHIS STATE TIGERS

	MIN	FGM-A	FTM-A	OFF	REB	AST	PF	PTS
Dewayne Bailey	21	1-2	0-0	1	5	0	1	2
Vincent Askew	37	0-1	1-2	0	1	1	1	1
William Bedford	24	4-5	4-4	2	4	2	4	12
Willie Becton	19	3-4	1-2	0	2	2	2	7
Andre Turner	40	5-9	2-5	0	3	12	3	12
	MIN	FGM-A	FTM-A	OFF	REB	AST	PF	PTS
Baskerville Holmes	21	2-4	0-0	2	4	0	1	4
Dwight Boyd	11	1-2	0-0	0	0	2	0	2
Keith Lee	27	9-22	5-5	3	11	0	4	23
TOTALS		FGM-A	FTM-A	OFF	REB	AST	PF	PTS
		25-49	13-18	8	30	19	16	63

OKLAHOMA SOONERS

	MIN	FGM-A	FTM-A	OFF	REB	AST	PF	PTS
Shawn Clark	3	0-1	0-0	0	0	0	0	0
Wayman Tisdale	40	5-10	1-1	1	12	4	3	11
Tim McCalister	39	6-12	2-2	0	0	5	5	14
Darryl Kennedy	38	7-15	2-2	2	5	3	3	16
Anthony Bowie	40	5-12	0-2	1	2	5	2	10
	MIN	FGM-A	FTM-A	OFF	REB	AST	PF	PTS
David Johnson	36	3-6	4-6	4	7	2	3	10
Linwood Davis	4	0-0	0-0	0	0	1	3	0
TOTALS		FGM-A	FTM-A	OFF	REB	AST	PF	PTS
		26-56	9-13	8	26	20	19	61

West Region

March 24

Denver, CO

1. St. John's 69

3. North Carolina State 60

It took 17 seasons and 12 trips to the NCAA tournament, but Lou Carnesecca finally had his taste of the Final Four. With five seconds remaining in the West regional final and victory assured, St. John's beloved coach let loose in an emotional display of hugs and high-fives with his players and assistants.

"After 1,000 games, this one … when I'm going down into the grave, this is the one I'll remember," an elated Carnesecca said after his third-ranked Redmen advanced to Lexington.

For much of the game it looked like Carnesecca's quest could come to a bitter end. While St. John's always seemed to be in control, North Carolina State repeatedly threatened in the final minutes to sneak off with the victory. The Wolfpack's Terry Gannon popped two jumpers to bring State within 51-48, but St. John's All-American Chris Mullin answered with a 3-point play and 15-foot shot to make the score 56-48. A short time later Mullin was called for his fourth foul, and then with 3:30 to play he was involved in a baseline collision that produced a whistle. For a brief, tense moment it appeared that Mullin might have fouled out, but the call went against the Pack. The Redmen breathed a sigh of relief and proceeded to sink six straight foul shots to amass a comfortable 65-55 lead and assure the school's first Final Four in 33 years.

The result might have been different if not for a controversial coaching move by N.C. State's Jim Valvano. Mullin's late scoring spree started after Valvano decided to put the 5-foot-7 Spud Webb on the 6-6 Mullin, saying that it was a "calculated risk" and "we weren't shooting well and we needed Gannon to shoot from the outside and Spud to penetrate."

"When you got a mismatch, obviously it's a natural thing to try to take advantage of it," Carnesecca said of Mullin first powering through Webb on his 3-point play and then shooting over him on the next possession. Valvano's switch to a smaller lineup was necessitated by St. John's defense collapsing on State's star center, Lorenzo Charles, who had erupted early in the second half for most of his team-high 15 points to lead his team to within 43-42 with 11:20 to play.

The pre-game chatter centered on the schools' loquacious coaches, who delighted the media with countless one-liners that were generally focused on their Italian heritage ("Mine is a used suit," Valvano said at one point. "I think somebody got blown away in it.") Making the game even more special were the family ties that Carnesecca and Valvano shared. Carnesecca's first game as a high school coach was against Valvano's father, Rocco, and Jimmy V's aunt was a nurse who helped deliver Carnesecca's daughter Enes.

The next stop for Looie and his Redmen was another family gathering of sorts at the Big East-dominated Final Four, starting with a semifinal showdown with hated rival Georgetown. "To beat Georgetown, you cannot afford to have an off day," said Carnesecca as he looked ahead to his fourth meeting of the season with the Hoyas. "In fact, a good day won't do. You need a great day."

ST. JOHN'S REDMEN								
	MIN	FGM-A	FTM-A	OFF	REB	AST	PF	PTS
Bill Wennington	36	3-5	8-9	-	10	0	2	14
Ron Stewart	19	1-3	5-7	-	3	1	0	7
Walter Berry	40	8-12	3-4	-	5	0	2	19
Mike Moses	22	1-4	2-3	-	2	5	2	4
Chris Mullin	40	9-19	7-7	-	5	1	4	25
	MIN	FGM-A	FTM-A	OFF	REB	AST	PF	PTS
Mark Jackson	19	0-1	0-1	-	3	5	4	0

		FGM-A	FTM-A	OFF	REB	AST	PF	PTS
Willie Glass	24	0-5	0-0	-	3	2	4	0
TOTALS		FGM-A	FTM-A	OFF	REB	AST	PF	PTS
		22-49	25-31	-	31	14	18	69

NORTH CAROLINA STATE WOLFPACK

	MIN	FGM-A	FTM-A	OFF	REB	AST	PF	PTS
Russell Pierre	25	3-6	0-0	-	3	0	5	6
Lorenzo Charles	39	4-9	7-9	-	11	1	2	15
Spud Webb	39	5-14	4-5	-	1	9	3	14
Cozell McQueen	40	2-4	4-6	-	11	1	4	8
Bennie Bolton	27	4-10	1-1	-	0	0	3	9
	MIN	FGM-A	FTM-A	OFF	REB	AST	PF	PTS
Terry Gannon	18	3-7	0-0	-	1	0	4	6
Nate McMillan	11	0-3	2-2	-	3	1	5	2
Ernie Myers	1	0-0	0-0	-	0	0	1	0
TOTALS		FGM-A	FTM-A	OFF	REB	AST	PF	PTS
		21-53	18-23	-	30	12	27	60

Southeast Region

March 24
Birmingham, AL
8. Villanova 56
2. North Carolina 44

For nearly 20 minutes, it looked like the clock was fast approaching midnight for the tournament's top remaining Cinderella. Then a chain of events occurred over seven seconds that changed the tide of the game, ultimately leading to another shocking upset in a March that had already seen its share of madness.

North Carolina, which had ground out a 22-14 lead, was holding the ball for the last shot of the opening half when Kenny Smith was called for traveling in the closing seconds. Villanova missed a shot but Dwayne McClain managed to tip in the rebound at the buzzer while also being fouled. He completed the 3-point play, and the Wildcats, who had been completely outplayed, joyfully swooped off the court down by only 5 after having made only 6 of 26 shots.

"At halftime we discussed what had gotten us this far, what we had gone through," Villanova coach Rollie Massimino said. "The only thing we changed was the players' thinking." That wasn't quite true. Massimino also made a change to his lineup, benching the 6-foot-1 Dwight Wilbur for 6-5 Harold Jensen, who proceeded to burn the Tar Heels with 10 second-half points as part of a startling turnaround.

Using a matchup zone that helped contain North Carolina's imposing big men while also making it hard for point guard Smith to get the ball, Villanova suffocated the Tar Heels and forced many sloppy turnovers that were converted into easy baskets. One such gimme happened with 16:30 to play when Harold Pressley swiped a crosscourt pass and laid in the points that gave the Wildcats a 27-26 lead that they would never give up. After their brutal first half, the Cats would make 16 of 21 shots in the final 20 minutes

"A combination of their defense and our offense," North Carolina coach Dean Smith said when asked what made the difference in the game. "We misfired on things we knew we could do. We threw passes I couldn't believe we threw." Smith grew visibly frustrated during his team's second-half meltdown, at one point giving a choke sign at an official for not calling a five-second violation against Villanova on an out-of-bounds play.

Jensen, Pressley and McClain each scored six points during a decisive 22-7 run that gave the Wildcats a commanding 43-33 lead with eight minutes remaining, all but wrapping up perhaps the biggest victory in the program's history. The emotional scene after the final horn included Massimino sharing tearful embraces with his son R.C. and point guard Gary McLain, Ed Pinckney standing triumphantly on top of the scorer's table with his arms raised and several players cutting down a net and placing it around the neck of Jake Nevin, their longtime trainer who was confined to a wheelchair with Lou Gehrig's Disease.

"We'll wear that glass slipper if you want, but we don't consider ourselves a Cinderella," Pinckney said. "I don't have to pinch myself anymore. This is reality."

NORTH CAROLINA TAR HEELS

	MIN	FGM-A	FTM-A	OFF	REB	AST	PF	PTS
Buzz Peterson	20	0-3	0-0	-	0	0	1	0
Dave Popson	14	2-3	1-1	-	2	0	0	5
Brad Daugherty	38	7-9	3-6	-	12	0	3	17
Joe Wolf	34	2-6	0-0	-	4	5	3	4
Kenny Smith	40	2-7	0-0	-	3	5	3	4
	MIN	FGM-A	FTM-A	OFF	REB	AST	PF	PTS
Ranzino Smith	20	3-10	0-0	-	4	0	2	6
Warren Martin	16	1-2	0-0	-	1	1	2	2
Curtis Hunter	16	3-4	0-0	-	2	0	2	6
Cliff Morris	2	0-0	0-0	-	0	0	0	0
TOTALS		FGM-A	FTM-A	OFF	REB	AST	PF	PTS
		20-44	4-7	-	28	11	16	44

VILLANOVA WILDCATS

	MIN	FGM-A	FTM-A	OFF	REB	AST	PF	PTS
Ed Pinckney	38	3-6	3-6	-	7	3	3	9
Mark Plansky	7	0-1	0-0	-	1	1	0	0

	MIN	FGM-A	FTM-A	OFF	REB	AST	PF	PTS
Harold Pressley	38	7-13	1-2	-	3	1	1	15
Dwight Wilbur	9	0-3	0-0	-	2	1	0	0
Dwayne McClain	36	4-11	3-3	-	5	2	3	11
	MIN	FGM-A	FTM-A	OFF	REB	AST	PF	PTS
Chuck Everson	2	0-1	0-0	-	0	0	1	0
Harold Jensen	31	5-7	0-0	-	3	3	1	10
Gary McLain	39	3-5	5-6	-	2	2	2	11
TOTALS		FGM-A	FTM-A	OFF	REB	AST	PF	PTS
		22-47	12-17	-	23	13	11	56

National Semifinals – Final Four

March 30
Lexington, KY
Villanova 52
Memphis State 45

The focus heading into the Final Four was on how a Big East party had broken out in the Bluegrass State, but the interloper from nearby Memphis seemed ready to prove that it could more than hold its own with the big boys from the East Coast. "There's great basketball played in the Big East but I think there's some great basketball played in our league, too," Memphis State coach Dana Kirk said. "I think it's biscuits and gravy versus bacon and sausage."

Villanova coach Rollie Massimino, meanwhile, bristled at once again being in the shadow of his conference brethren. His Wildcats, who finished third in the Big East, had been the darlings of the NCAA tournament but were given little chance of emerging on top from a quartet that included Big East rivals Georgetown and St. John's, against whom the Cats had been a combined 0-5 in 1984-85. "Hey, there's two other teams here," Massimino noted two days before the Final Four. Still, the consensus was that the other semifinal between the Hoyas and Redmen would be the "real" championship game.

If Villanova was indeed just playing for second place, it took its task very seriously. The Wildcats worked their typical methodical, hard-nosed, smart and opportunistic style of play to perfection against the Tigers by containing Memphis State's cat-quick point guard Andre Turner while aggressively attacking the Tigers' towering duo of William Bedford and Keith Lee until foul trouble turned the pair into a non-factor. "We look bad, but we make the other team look worse," said Harold Pressley of his Villanova team that was being chided for "winning ugly". "Our plan is to frustrate the other team as much as possible with our offense and with our defense. We did it to Memphis State both ways."

A key stretch early in the second half epitomized the day for both teams. With Memphis State holding a 31-28 lead, Villanova embarked on a nine-point run that caused the Tigers to completely unravel. At one point Bedford, upset at a traveling call, hurled the ball away and was slapped with a technical foul.

Twenty seconds later he then foolishly fouled Pressley after a rebound, and minutes later the All-American Lee fouled out of the game while pursuing a loose ball that he had no chance to get. Suddenly, the Tigers were down 41-33 and in desperation mode.

After the game, the frustrated Tigers would have no trouble pointing fingers and making excuses. The focus of their wrath was the officials. "I don't know what's going on. It's amazing," said Lee, who had played only 23 minutes and scored 10 points before fouling out (he had also fouled out three years earlier in an overtime loss to Villanova in the NCAA tournament). "We barely touch someone and we get a foul. I don't think we played a bad game. The refs just didn't let us play. What do they have against Memphis State?"

Still, just when the Tigers looked finished, the Wildcats suddenly lost their way. With Lee out of the game, Memphis State was forced to use a smaller lineup that wound up frustrating Villanova, which went 7:17 without scoring a point as its eight-point lead was reduced to zero. "We let down a little bit. They couldn't believe it (the eight-point edge) at the time. We got a little complacent," Massimino explained.

But as they had done all tournament, the senior-laden Wildcats kept their poise. Dwayne McClain, who would make 24 of 25 free throw attempts in the tournament, including all 7 in this game, sank a pair with 3 minutes left that gave Villanova the lead for good at 43-41. The cagey Cats got away with sending McClain to the line when in fact it was Pressley who had been fouled. "I could've used the two points," Pressley joked. "But Dwayne has been shooting outstandingly in the tournament so I let him do it."

McClain administered the coup de grace a minute later with a powerful dunk off a baseline drive that boosted the lead to four and prompted the Cats to go to their spread offense to work the clock and protect their lead. "I look forward to the (shot) clock next year. I think the fans want to be entertained more," Kirk griped.

Other Tigers besides Lee took shots at the officiating after the game. "A lot of the fouls we thought weren't fouls," Baskerville Holmes said. "The refs called a very poor game. They say the Big East is such a touch conference. If they're so tough, why do the referees protect them?" Kirk added: "They talk about the aggressive style of play in the Big East and how timid we are in the Metro Conference. Yet they shoot 26 foul shots to our 9."

Villanova's Ed Pinckney stated that getting the Tigers in foul trouble was his team's plan all along. "We knew Lee had been in foul trouble during the tournament," he said. "So we tried to take the ball to him as much as we could."

Whether Villanova got a boost from the refs or not, one of the most improbable stories in NCAA basketball history would receive one more chapter with the championship game on April Fools' Day. But Kirk, for one, was seeing the rugged and resourceful Wildcats in a new light. "If they're a Cinderella team," he said, "then Cinderella wears boots."

VILLANOVA WILDCATS

	MIN	FGM-A	FTM-A	OFF	REB	AST	PF	PTS
Ed Pinckney	-	3-7	6-9	3	9	1	3	12
Mark Plansky	-	1-1	1-3	0	0	2	1	3
Harold Pressley	-	1-8	1-2	4	6	1	3	3
Dwight Wilbur	-	0-2	0-0	1	1	0	1	0
Dwayne McClain	-	6-9	7-7	0	4	2	4	19
	MIN	FGM-A	FTM-A	OFF	REB	AST	PF	PTS
Chuck Everson	-	0-0	0-0	0	0	0	0	0
Harold Jensen	-	3-6	0-0	0	4	1	0	6
Gary McLain	-	2-5	5-5	0	2	2	1	9
TOTALS		FGM-A	FTM-A	OFF	REB	AST	PF	PTS
		16-38	20-26	8	26	9	13	52

MEMPHIS STATE TIGERS

	MIN	FGM-A	FTM-A	OFF	REB	AST	PF	PTS
Dewayne Bailey	8	1-1	0-0	0	0	0	2	2
Vincent Askew	40	1-3	0-1	6	7	7	2	2
William Bedford	32	4-9	0-0	3	7	0	4	8
Willie Becton	22	1-4	2-2	1	5	1	1	4
Andre Turner	40	5-13	1-2	0	4	3	3	11
	MIN	FGM-A	FTM-A	OFF	REB	AST	PF	PTS
John Wilfong	1	0-1	0-0	1	1	0	1	0
Baskerville Holmes	31	4-8	0-0	2	2	0	5	8
Dwight Boyd	3	0-2	0-0	0	0	0	0	0
Keith Lee	23	3-9	4-4	0	7	1	5	10
TOTALS		FGM-A	FTM-A	OFF	REB	AST	PF	PTS
		19-50	7-9	13	33	12	23	45

Georgetown 77
St. John's 59

After Georgetown's latest 40 minutes of brilliantly bruising basketball, the question wasn't so much whether the Hoyas would go on to win their second straight national title but where they ranked among the greatest teams in NCAA history.

"I would have to compare them to the great teams of San Francisco with Bill Russell, the great Kentucky teams of the past, the UCLA clubs and, of course, the Indiana team with the five pros," said St. John's coach Lou Carnesecca after his third-ranked Redmen had endured their third straight blowout loss to the Hoyas. "When a club executes as well as they do and plays at such a level of proficiency, there is really nothing you can do."

Superlatives were in order after Georgetown's complete dismantling of a team that lost only four times all season – the last three to the Hoyas by an average margin of 15 points. The famed "Hoya Paranoia" defense was at its best, with David Wingate stuck to St. John's All-American Chris Mullin like glue as part of a box-and-one defense that Georgetown had used effectively against the Redmen in their earlier meetings. Mullin, who had averaged 25.5 points per game in the NCAA tournament, was held to 8, including zero in a second half in which he attempted just three shots. Mullin's measly output ended his streak of 101 straight games in double figures and came in his final game in a St. John's uniform.

"Theirs is possibly the toughest defense to penetrate against. It gets frustrating," Mullin said. "If I can, I just try to keep my man occupied. It may not look like I'm doing anything, but I'm trying."

While Wingate was occupied with Mullin, his Hoya teammates were producing with lethal efficiency on the offensive end. The Big East champs jumped out to an 18-8 lead behind Reggie Williams, who scored 10 points in the first half and would finish with a game-high 20. But when Patrick Ewing headed to the bench after his second foul, St. John's found the going easier. Center Bill Wennington stepped up with Mullin struggling and scored 10 points, and a Mullin jumper capped a 10-0 run that knotted the score at 26.

But Georgetown would soon take the lead for good and then start the second half with a 7-point burst. The swarming, relentless Hoya defense and the Redmen's own sloppiness (they would finish with 18 turnovers to 7 for Georgetown) made another rally impossible and St. John's would never get closer than 9 points for the remainder of the game. After a Willie Glass 3-point play cut their lead to 62-51, the Hoyas turned to their spread offense to milk the clock, forcing St. John's to foul. Georgetown took care of business at the free throw line, making 19 of 24 attempts on the day, as this much-anticipated meeting of the only two teams to be ranked No. 1 in 1984-85 turned into a snooze.

Carnesecca summed up the rout by saying, "We tried everything against them. It just didn't work." His counterpart, John Thompson, was his usual cautious self, even though his team had just won its 10th straight NCAA tournament game. "It's a little too early to be pleased," he said. "There is one more ballgame to be played. I get pleased after we are out of here. I get some rest, too."

And while most observers were already crowning Georgetown as champions, Wennington for one saw at least a glimmer of hope for the Hoyas' final foe, Villanova. "I think if Villanova plays like they did today, taking the ball inside the way they did, they can get some people into foul trouble and make a ball game of it," he observed. But a decent game seemed to be the most that basketball fans could hope for from a championship matchup that looked like a mismatch.

GEORGETOWN HOYAS

	MIN	FGM-A	FTM-A	OFF	REB	AST	PF	PTS
Ralph Dalton	17	2-2	0-0	0	1	0	3	4
Reggie Williams	33	8-15	4-4	4	4	2	1	20
David Wingate	36	3-8	6-8	3	6	2	2	12
Kevin Floyd	1	0-0	0-0	1	1	0	0	0
Bill Martin	29	4-8	4-4	4	7	0	4	12
	MIN	FGM-A	FTM-A	OFF	REB	AST	PF	PTS
Grady Mateen	3	0-1	0-0	0	0	0	0	0
Perry McDonald	3	0-1	0-0	0	1	0	0	0
Ralph Highsmith	1	0-1	0-0	1	1	0	0	0
Tyrone Lockhart	1	0-0	0-0	0	0	0	0	0
Patrick Ewing	32	7-12	2-4	1	5	2	4	16
Horace Broadnax	20	3-4	3-4	2	3	1	0	9
Michael Jackson	24	2-5	0-0	0	0	11	4	4
TOTALS		FGM-A	FTM-A	OFF	REB	AST	PF	PTS
		29-57	19-24	16	29	18	18	77

ST. JOHN'S REDMEN

	MIN	FGM-A	FTM-A	OFF	REB	AST	PF	PTS
Bill Wennington	38	4-7	4-5	2	5	0	2	12
Rob Cornegy	1	0-0	0-0	0	1	0	0	0
Steve Shurina	2	0-0	0-0	0	0	0	0	0
Ron Stewart	6	0-0	0-0	0	0	0	2	0
Walter Berry	37	4-8	4-5	2	6	3	4	12
	MIN	FGM-A	FTM-A	OFF	REB	AST	PF	PTS
Terry Bross	1	0-0	0-0	0	0	0	1	0
Mike Moses	17	3-7	0-0	0	1	2	3	6
Chris Mullin	39	4-8	0-0	1	5	1	2	8
Mark Jackson	22	3-4	0-2	1	2	5	1	6
Shelton Jones	12	1-4	0-0	1	2	1	1	2
Willie Glass	25	4-4	5-7	2	2	0	4	13
TOTALS		FGM-A	FTM-A	OFF	REB	AST	PF	PTS
		23-42	13-19	9	24	12	20	59

National Championship Game

April 1
Lexington, KY
Villanova 66
Georgetown 64

"We're going to have to play a perfect game."

Even Villanova coach Rollie Massimino seemed skeptical of his team's chances of rocking the college basketball world by upsetting the seemingly invincible Hoyas. Sure, the Wildcats had gone toe-to-toe with the Hoyas in two close regular-season meetings, losing both by a combined nine points. And there was no denying that Villanova came into the final game on a major roll, defeating the nation's No. 2 (Michigan) and No. 5 (Memphis State) teams while playing its brand of tough, opportunistic basketball to perfection.

But still, Georgetown had been so utterly awesome all season, especially in its previous game, an 18-point annihilation of third-ranked St. John's, that few thought the Wildcats' magical run would last one more game. Even the Las Vegas oddsmakers pegged the Hoyas as a 9-point favorite. Because a Georgetown win seemed like a guarantee, much of the pre-game talk centered on where this Hoyas team ranked among the all-time championship teams, including the UCLA Bruins of John Wooden, who were the last repeat champs in 1973. Even Massimino was in awe: "They are the No. 1 team in the United States and probably one of the best teams ever assembled in the history of college basketball."

But on this April Fools' Day, the joke would be on the so-called experts. The Wildcats did not play the "perfect game" that Massimino sought, but they were pretty darn close. They made 78.6 percent of their shots, including 9 of 10 in the second half, against the nation's top-ranked defense. Point guard Gary McLain played all 40 minutes and only turned the ball over twice against Georgetown's relentless pressure defense. Ed Pinckney more than held his own against the fearsome Patrick Ewing, producing 16 points, 6 rebounds and 5 assists to Ewing's 14, 5 and 2 and wrapping up the tournament's Most Outstanding Player award.

From the outset, the Hoyas dipped into their notorious bag of intimidation tricks, with Reggie Williams telling Dwayne McClain that he was going to "kick your butt" and Michael Jackson sticking his finger in McLain's face after a turnover. Williams even took a swipe at Villanova's Chuck Everson at the end of the first half. But the Wildcats never retaliated or lost their cool. "That's not classy," McLain said of the incidents. "The classy program was going to win this championship. We're very classy."

Villanova was also lucky in the sense that this was the last NCAA tournament to be played without a shot clock. In their earlier losses to the Hoyas, the Wildcats had sometimes been pressured into taking poor shots thanks in part to the Big East conference's 45-second clock. But in the final, as during the enter tourney, the Cats thrived without the constraint of a clock, patiently probing for good looks in their spread offense and frustrating Georgetown into 22 fouls. Villanova capitalized by making 19 of 23 free throws in the second half.

Despite all they did right, it still almost wasn't enough for the Wildcats. Georgetown demonstrated why it was considered an all-time great in going 35-2 on the season by sticking close to its inspired opponent. Both teams got off to a blazing start, with Villanova making seven of its first eight shots but still trailing 20-14 thanks in part to eight quick points by Williams. Georgetown coach John Thompson then made the questionable decision to take out the red-hot Williams, saying that he "was winded." Williams seemed to lose his touch and was held scoreless in the second half.

Early in the second half, Villanova took a 6-point lead and still held a 53-48 edge before Georgetown snapped back. When David Wingate drained a 14-foot jumper with 4:50 left to give the Hoyas a 54-53 lead, it seemed that their 18th straight win and second consecutive national title were near. But Bill Martin threw the ball away with 3:30 remaining after the Hoyas had gone into their own spread offense in order to milk the clock, setting the stage for perhaps Villanova's most unlikely of heroes.

Harold Jensen, an often overlooked backup guard, coolly sank an 18-footer from the right wing with 2:35 on the clock to give Villanova the lead for good at 55-54. "If I'm wide open, Coach (Massimino) always tells me to put the ball up in that situation. And, fortunately, it went," said Jensen, who made all five of his shots and four of five free throws after averaging only 4.5 points per game during the season.

Villanova's deadly shooting extended to the free throw line, from where the Cats scored 11 points down the stretch. Jensen himself twice sank both ends of one-and-one situations, helping Villanova build a 61-54 lead with 1:10 remaining. Before he attempted his second one-and-one, Jensen kissed the bald head of 78-year-old wheelchair-bound trainer Jake Nevin, who was battling Lou Gehrig's Disease and had become a fixture on the Villanova bench during the tournament. "This one's for you," Jensen told him.

Jackson's layup with five seconds to go cut the Hoyas' deficit to two, but since Georgetown had no more timeouts it appeared that Villanova would not need to inbound the ball before time ran out. However, a quick-thinking Wingate knocked the ball into the stands and the officials, instead of calling a technical foul, merely stopped the clock. As the Wildcats tried to throw the ball in, McClain was knocked to the floor but Jensen inbounded the ball to him anyway. The senior clutched the ball until the clock showed all zeroes, touching off a wild celebration. "This is awesome – as everyone said Georgetown was this morning," McClain crowed amidst the jubilation. "It's not a miracle to me," Pinckney said. "I knew we could win all along."

The Hoyas remained feisty, even in defeat. "We might not have won the ball game, but I still think we're No. 1," said Ewing, who struggled with Villanova's 2-3 matchup zone and got off only one shot in the game's final 13 minutes. Thompson was gracious in defeat, saying, "Look at their percentages both from the field and the free throw line. Villanova won the game fairly. We have no complaints."

Fans of basketball weren't complaining, either, after they had witnessed one of the great upsets in the sport's history, performed by a team of overachievers who had played the game of their lives. Hours before the game, Massimino had sent his players to their hotel rooms for 15 minutes to, in his words, "think about two things. One, play with the idea to win, not of losing. Two, tell yourselves you're good enough to win. In a one-shot deal, you are good enough to beat anybody." Villanova turned the power of positive thinking into a near-perfect performance that would stamp them for all time as the kings of the Cinderellas.

GEORGETOWN HOYAS

	MIN	FGM-A	FTM-A	OFF	REB	AST	PF	PTS
Ralph Dalton	4	0-1	2-2	0	0	0	1	2
Reggie Williams	29	5-9	0-2	4	4	2	3	10
David Wingate	39	8-14	0-0	1	2	2	4	16
Bill Martin	37	4-6	2-2	3	5	1	2	10
Perry McDonald	2	0-1	0-0	0	0	0	0	0
	MIN	FGM-A	FTM-A	OFF	REB	AST	PF	PTS
Patrick Ewing	39	7-13	0-0	2	5	2	4	14
Horace Broadnax	13	1-2	2-2	0	1	2	4	4
Michael Jackson	37	4-7	0-0	0	0	9	4	8
TOTALS		FGM-A	FTM-A	OFF	REB	AST	PF	PTS
		29-53	6-8	10	17	18	22	64

VILLANOVA WILDCATS

	MIN	FGM-A	FTM-A	OFF	REB	AST	PF	PTS
Ed Pinckney	37	5-7	6-7	1	6	5	3	16
Mark Plansky	1	0-0	0-1	0	0	0	1	0
Harold Pressley	40	4-6	3-4	1	4	1	1	11
Dwight Wilbur	5	0-0	0-0	0	0	1	0	0
Dwayne McClain	40	5-7	7-8	0	1	3	3	17
	MIN	FGM-A	FTM-A	OFF	REB	AST	PF	PTS
Chuck Everson	3	0-0	0-0	0	0	0	0	0
Harold Jensen	34	5-5	4-5	0	1	2	2	14
Gary McLain	40	3-3	2-2	0	2	2	2	8
TOTALS		FGM-A	FTM-A	OFF	REB	AST	PF	PTS
		22-28	22-27	2	14	14	12	66

1985 NCAA Tournament Most Outstanding Player
Ed Pinckney, Center, Villanova

One of the senior leaders on Villanova's championship once was set on attending a different college before he got some surprising advice. Pinckney was ready to commit to Providence when the Friars' coach, Gary Walters, told him, "Ed, you'll be better off going to Villanova. I think Providence is a fine school and a terrific place, but I think you'll do better at Villanova." Fortunately for Villanova, Pinckney heeded Walters, and his college journey ended with one of the most unforgettable upsets in basketball history.

Pinckney arrived on Villanova's Main Line campus in 1981 as part of a heralded recruiting class that included Dwayne McClain and Gary McLain. The three bonded quickly and vowed to return the Wildcats program to glory by leading the team to a Final Four. They came up just one step short in each of their first two years, losing in the regional finals, before finally breaking through on their last try in 1985.

The Wildcats did not exactly enter the NCAA tournament on a high note. They lost 7 of their final 13 games, including a 23-point drubbing at the hands of Pittsburgh in the regular-season finale. But it was in a rematch with the Panthers five days later in the quarterfinals of the Big East tournament that "E-Z Ed" made one of his most important plays. After Pitt had jumped out to a quick eight-point lead, Joey David was swooping in for what looked like a cinch layup when Pinckney hustled over and blocked the shot. The Wildcats regrouped after that and went on to win 69-61.

"Incredible play," Villanova coach Rollie Massimino said. "Just the fact he hustled back was impressive, but then he makes the block besides. That's what you call leading by example."

That's the kind of leadership Pinckney provided throughout the Wildcats' magical run to the NCAA championship. He averaged 14.5 points on 59 percent shooting and 8 rebounds in Villanova's six tourney games while facing a who's-who of the game's best big men – Roy Tarpley, Len Bias, Brad Daugherty, Keith Lee, William Bedford and Patrick Ewing – all of whom would be drafted within the top 11 by the NBA. Pinckney himself would be selected 10th overall by the Phoenix Suns in 1985 and he enjoyed a 12-year professional career.

His crowning glory, however, will always be the 1985 final in which he outplayed Georgetown All-American Ewing. Just don't make the mistake of calling it his best game ever. As Pinckney noted at the time, "My greatest game was two years ago – 27 points, 22 rebounds – against Georgetown."

All-Tournament Team

Ed Pinckney, C, Villanova – 14.5 PPG, 8.0 RPG
Patrick Ewing, C, Georgetown – 14.7 PPG, 6.5 RPG
Harold Jensen, G, Villanova – 6.8 PPG
Dwayne McClain, F, Villanova – 15.0 PPG, 3.8 RPG
Gary McLain, G, Villanova – 7.0 PPG

Individual Statistical Leaders

Scoring

Most points, single game

1. Sam Vincent, Michigan State (vs. Alabama-Birmingham) – 32
1. Mark Davis, Old Dominion (vs. SMU) – 32
3. Steve Harris, Tulsa (vs. UTEP) – 31

Most total points, tournament

1. Chris Mullin, St. John's – 110
2. Lorenzo Charles, North Carolina State – 103
3. Walter Berry, St. John's – 93
4. Wayman Tisdale, Oklahoma – 91
5. Dwayne McClain, Villanova – 90

Highest scoring average (minimum 2 games)

1. Rolando Lamb, Virginia Commonwealth – 27.5
2. Kenny Walker, Kentucky – 25.0
3. Joe Kleine, Arkansas – 24.0
4. Wayman Tisdale, Oklahoma – 22.8
5. Luster Goodwin, UTEP – 22.5

Field Goals

Most field goals, single game

1. Wayman Tisdale, Oklahoma (vs. Illinois State) – 14
1. Mark Davis, Old Dominion (vs. SMU) – 14
3. Sam Vincent, Michigan State (vs. Alabama-Birmingham) – 13

Most total field goals, tournament

1. Wayman Tisdale, Oklahoma – 41
2. Chris Mullin, St. John's – 39
3. Lorenzo Charles, North Carolina State – 37
4. Andre Turner, Memphis State – 35
4. Patrick Ewing, Georgetown – 35

Most field goal attempts, single game

1. Reggie Lewis, Northeastern (vs. Illinois) – 28
2. Chuck Person, Auburn (vs. North Carolina) – 25
3. Barry Stevens, Iowa State (vs. Ohio State) – 24

Most total field goal attempts, tournament

1. Chris Mullin, St. John's – 77
2. Keith Lee, Memphis State – 68
3. Andre Turner, Memphis State – 65
4. Patrick Ewing, Georgetown – 64
5. Lorenzo Charles, North Carolina State – 63

Highest field goal percentage, single game (minimum 10 attempts)

1. Wayman Tisdale, Oklahoma (vs. Illinois State) -- .875 (14 of 16)
2. Bill Wennington, St. John's (vs. Southern) -- .833 (10 of 12)
3. Lorenzo Charles, North Carolina State (vs. UTEP) -- .800 (12 of 15)
3. Leonard Allen, San Diego State (vs. UNLV) -- .800 (8 of 10)
3. Bobby Lee Hurt, Alabama (vs. Virginia Commonwealth) -- .800 (8 of 10)

Highest field goal percentage, tournament (minimum 20 attempts)

1. Brad Daugherty, North Carolina -- .725 (29 of 40)
2. Ken Norman, Illinois -- .720 (18 of 25)
3. Frank Ford, Auburn -- .700 (21 of 30)
4. Wayman Tisdale, Oklahoma -- .695 (41 of 59)
5. Bill Wennington, St. John's -- .686 (24 of 35)

Free Throws

Most free throws made, single game

1. Dwayne Washington, Syracuse (vs. DePaul) – 15
2. Spud Webb, North Carolina State (vs. UTEP) – 13
2. Kenny Walker, Kentucky (vs. Washington) –13

Most total free throws made, tournament

1. Ed Pinckney, Villanova – 39
2. Chris Mullin, St. John's – 32
3. Lorenzo Charles, North Carolina State – 29
4. Spud Webb, North Carolina State – 27
5. Walter Berry, St. John's – 25

Most free throws attempted, single game

1. Spud Webb, North Carolina State (vs. UTEP) – 17
2. Dwayne Washington, Syracuse (vs. DePaul) – 16
3. Kenny Walker, Kentucky (vs. Washington) – 15
4. David Henderson, Duke (vs. Pepperdine) – 14

Most free throws attempted, tournament

1. Ed Pinckney, Villanova – 53
2. Lorenzo Charles, North Carolina State – 39
3. Chris Mullin, St. John's – 37
4. Spud Webb, North Carolina State – 36
5. Walter Berry, St. John's – 32

Highest free throw percentage, single game (minimum 7 attempts)

1. Chris Mullin, St. John's (vs. Arkansas) – 1.000 (10 of 10)
1. Vernon Butler, Navy (vs. LSU) – 1.000 (10 of 10)
1. Gary Wilson, Fairleigh Dickinson (vs. Michigan) – 1.000 (8 of 8)
1. Damon Goodwin, Dayton (vs. Villanova) – 1.000 (8 of 8)
1. Doug Wojcik, Navy (vs. LSU) – 1.000 (8 of 8)

Highest free throw percentage, tournament (minimum 15 attempts)

1. Dwayne McClain, Villanova -- .960 (24 of 25)
2. Vernon Butler, Navy -- .933 (14 of 15)
3. Dwayne Washington, Syracuse -- .900 (18 of 20)
4. James Ponder, Alabama-Birmingham -- .895 (17 of 19)
5. Chris Mullin, St. John's -- .865 (32 of 37)

Rebounds

Most rebounds, single game

1. David Robinson, Navy (vs. LSU) – 18
2. Bob Coleman, Iona (vs. Loyola (IL)) – 16
2. Karl Malone, Louisiana Tech (vs. Oklahoma) – 16
4. Anthony Gordon, Alabama-Birmingham (vs. Memphis State) – 15
4. Larry Davis, SMU (vs. Old Dominion) – 15

Most total rebounds, tournament

1. Lorenzo Charles, North Carolina State – 51
2. Ed Pinckney, Villanova – 48
3. Wayman Tisdale, Oklahoma – 43

3. Brad Daugherty, North Carolina – 43

5. Walter Berry, St. John's – 42

Most rebounds per game (minimum 2 games)

1. Karl Malone, Louisiana Tech – 13.3 (40 in 3 games)
2. Roy Tarpley, Michigan – 13.0 (26 in 2 games)
2. David Robinson, Navy – 13.0 (26 in 2 games)
4. Joe Kleine, Arkansas – 12.5 (25 in 2 games)
5. Larry Davis, SMU – 12.0 (24 in 2 games)

Assists

Most assists, single game

1. Kenny Patterson, DePaul (vs. Syracuse) – 15
2. Carl Golston, Loyola (IL) (vs. Iona) – 12
2. Andre Turner, Memphis State (vs. Oklahoma) – 12
2. Michael Jackson, Georgetown (vs. Loyola (IL)) – 12
2. Keith Gatlin, Maryland (vs. Navy) – 12

Most total assists, tournament

1. Michael Jackson, Georgetown – 45
2. Andre Turner, Memphis State – 38
3. Spud Webb, North Carolina State – 29
4. Vincent Askew, Memphis State – 27
5. Wayne Smith, Louisiana Tech – 26

Most assists per game (minimum 2 games)

1. Butch Moore, SMU – 9.5 (19 in 2 games)
2. Wayne Smith, Louisiana Tech – 8.67 (26 in 3 games)
3. Carl Golston, Loyola (IL) – 8.0 (24 in 3 games)
3. Keith Gatlin, Maryland – 8.0 (24 in 3 games)
5. Andre Turner, Memphis State – 7.6 (38 in 5 games)

Turnovers

Most turnovers, single game

1. Bruce Douglas, Illinois (vs. Georgia Tech) – 9
2. Detlef Schrempf, Washington (vs. Kentucky) – 8
3. Anthony Bowie, Oklahoma (vs. Memphis State) – 7
3. Barry Stevens, Iowa State (vs. Ohio State) – 7
3. Chris Mullin, St. John's (vs. Southern) – 7

Most total turnovers, tournament

1. Chris Mullin, St. John's – 20
2. Dwayne McClain, Villanova – 19
3. Spud Webb, North Carolina State – 17
3. Bruce Douglas, Illinois – 17

Shots Blocked

Most shots blocked, single game

1. Warren Martin, North Carolina (vs. Middle Tennessee State) – 6
1. Patrick Ewing, Georgetown (vs. Lehigh) – 6
3. Patrick Ewing, Georgetown (vs. Loyola (IL)) – 5

Most total shots blocked, tournament

1. Patrick Ewing, Georgetown – 13
2. Ed Pinckney, Villanova – 10
3. Warren Martin, North Carolina – 9
3. William Bedford, Memphis State – 9

Steals

Most steals, single game

1. Rolando Lamb, Virginia Commonwealth (vs. Marshall) – 6
1. Bruce Douglas, Illinois (vs. Georgia) – 6
3. Willie Bland, Louisiana Tech (vs. Oklahoma) – 5
3. Daryl Shepherd, Pittsburgh (vs. Louisiana Tech) – 5
3. Harold Pressley, Villanova (vs. Michigan) – 5

Most total steals, tournament

1. Harold Pressley, Villanova – 15
2. Chris Mullin, St. John's – 11
3. Rolando Lamb, Virginia Commonwealth – 9

Team Statistical Leaders

Scoring

Most points, single game

1. Oklahoma (vs. North Carolina A&T) – 96
2. Three tied – 86

Most total points, tournament

1. Georgetown – 397
2. St. John's – 365
3. Villanova – 330

Highest scoring average (minimum 2 games)

1. Louisiana Tech – 80.3 (241 points in 3 games)
2. Oklahoma – 79.5 (318 points in 4 games)
3. UTEP – 76.0 (152 points in 2 games)

Field Goals

Most field goals, single game

1. Oklahoma (vs. North Carolina A&T) – 39
2. SMU (vs. Old Dominion) – 38
3. Oklahoma (vs. Louisiana Tech) – 37

Most total field goals, tournament

1. Georgetown – 152
2. Oklahoma – 137
3. Memphis State – 129

Most field goals attempted, single game

1. Louisiana Tech (vs. Oklahoma) – 84
2. Old Dominion (vs. SMU) – 77
3. Oklahoma (vs. North Carolina A&T) – 74

Most field goals attempted, tournament

1. Georgetown – 305
2. Memphis State – 269
3. Oklahoma – 250

Highest field goal percentage, single game

1. Villanova (vs. Georgetown) -- .786 (22 of 28)
2. North Carolina State (vs. UTEP) -- .732 (30 of 41)
3. Oklahoma (vs. Illinois State) -- .660 (35 of 53)

Highest field goal percentage, tournament (minimum 2 games)

1. Notre Dame -- .565 (52 of 92)
2. Oklahoma -- .548 (137 of 250)

Free Throws

Most free throws, single game

1. UTEP (vs. Tulsa) – 39
2. Navy (vs. LSU) – 34
3. Kentucky (vs. Washington) – 30

Most total free throws, tournament

1. St. John's – 109
2. Villanova – 102
3. Georgetown – 93

Most free throws attempted, single game

1. UTEP (vs. Tulsa) – 55
2. Navy (vs. LSU) – 43

Most total free throws attempted, tournament

1. St. John's – 143
2. Georgetown – 137
3. Villanova – 136

Highest free throw percentage, single game

1. Dayton (vs. Villanova) – 1.000 (17 of 17)
2. Lehigh (vs. Georgetown) -- .938 (15 of 16)
3. Georgia Tech (vs. Georgetown) -- .917 (22 of 24)

Highest free throw percentage, tournament (minimum 2 games)

1. Maryland -- .824 (28 of 34)
2. Georgia Tech -- .768 (86 of 112)
3. Illinois State -- .767 (23 of 30)

Lowest free throw percentage, single game

1. Washington (vs. Kentucky) -- .375 (6 of 16)
2. Virginia Commonwealth (vs. Alabama) -- .385 (5 of 13)
3. Iowa (vs. Arkansas) -- .400 (6 of 15)

Lowest free throw percentage, tournament (minimum 2 games)

1. SMU -- .560 (14 of 25)
2. Georgia -- .567 (17 of 30)
3. Kansas -- .600 (21 of 35)

Rebounds

Most rebounds, single game

1. Louisiana Tech (vs. Pittsburgh) – 51
2. Three tied – 42

Most rebounds per game (minimum 2 games)

1. Louisiana Tech – 43.3 (130 in 3 games)
2. SMU – 42.0 (84 in 2 games)
3. Duke – 36.5 (73 in 2 games)

Assists

Most assists, single game

1. Louisiana Tech (vs. Oklahoma) – 26
2. Oklahoma (vs. North Carolina A&T) – 24
2. Oklahoma (vs. Illinois State) – 24

Most assists per game (minimum 2 games)

1. Louisiana Tech – 21.7 (65 in 3 games)
2. Oklahoma – 21.5 (86 in 4 games)
2. SMU – 21.5 (43 in 2 games)

Turnovers

Most turnovers, single game

1. Northeastern (vs. Illinois) – 20
1. Marshall (vs. Virginia Commonwealth) – 20
3. Three tied – 19

Most turnovers per game (minimum 2 games)

1. Illinois – 17.3 (52 in 3 games)
2. SMU – 17.0 (34 in 2 games)
3. Georgia Tech – 15.0 (60 in 4 games)

Shots Blocked

Most shots blocked, single game

1. North Carolina (vs. Middle Tennessee State) – 10
2. Georgetown (vs. Lehigh) – 9
3. Two tied – 8

Most shots blocked per game (minimum 2 games)

1. Alabama – 4.7 (14 in 3 games)
2. North Carolina – 4.5 (18 in 4 games)

Steals

Most steals, single game

1. Villanova (vs. North Carolina) – 13
2. Louisiana Tech (vs. Oklahoma) – 11
2. Georgia Tech (vs. Illinois) – 11
2. Mercer (vs. Georgia Tech) – 11
2. Virginia Commonwealth (vs. Marshall) – 11

Most steals per game

1. Illinois – 8.7 (26 in 3 games)
2. Georgia – 8.5 (17 in 2 games)
3. Louisiana Tech – 7.7 (23 in 3 games)

1984-85 Conference Standings

	AMCU-8	
	Conference record	Overall record
Cleveland State	11-3	21-8
Western Illinois	10-4	14-14
Eastern Illinois	9-5	20-10
Missouri State	8-6	17-13
Illinois-Chicago	7-7	14-14
Northern Iowa	6-8	12-16
Valparaiso	4-10	8-20
Wisconsin-Green Bay	1-13	4-24
Tournament: Eastern Illinois over Missouri State, 75-64		

	Atlantic 10	
	Conference record	Overall record
West Virginia	16-2	20-9
Temple	15-3	25-6
Saint Joseph's	13-5	19-12
Rutgers	9-9	16-14
George Washington	9-9	14-14
Massachusetts	9-9	13-15
St. Bonaventure	7-11	14-15
Duquesne	6-12	12-18
Penn State	4-14	8-19
Rhode Island	2-16	8-20
Tournament: Temple over Rutgers, 59-51		

	ACC	
	Conference record	Overall record
Georgia Tech	9-5	27-8
North Carolina	9-5	27-9
North Carolina State	9-5	23-10
Duke	8-6	23-8
Maryland	8-6	25-12
Clemson	5-9	16-13
Wake Forest	5-9	15-14
Virginia	3-11	17-16
Tournament: Georgia Tech over North Carolina, 57-54		

	Big East	
	Conference record	Overall record
St. John's	15-1	31-4
Georgetown	14-2	35-3
Villanova	9-7	25-10
Syracuse	9-7	22-9
Pittsburgh	8-8	17-12
Boston College	7-9	20-11
Connecticut	6-10	13-15
Providence	3-13	11-20
Seton Hall	1-15	10-18
Tournament: Georgetown over St. John's, 92-80		

	Big Eight	
	Conference record	Overall record
Oklahoma	13-1	31-6
Kansas	11-3	26-8
Iowa State	7-7	21-13
Missouri	7-7	18-14
Nebraska	5-9	16-14
Kansas State	5-9	14-14
Colorado	5-9	11-17
Oklahoma State	3-11	12-16
Tournament: Oklahoma over Iowa State, 73-71		

	Big Sky	
	Conference record	Overall record
Nevada	11-3	21-10
Montana	10-4	22-8
Weber State	9-5	20-9
Northern Arizona	8-6	17-12
Montana State	7-7	11-17
Boise State	5-9	16-13
Idaho State	5-9	15-18
Idaho	1-13	8-22
Tournament: Nevada over Idaho State, 79-63		

	Big Ten	
	Conference record	Overall record
Michigan	16-2	26-4
Illinois	12-6	26-9
Purdue	11-7	20-9
Ohio State	11-7	20-10
Iowa	10-8	21-11
Michigan State	10-8	19-10
Indiana	7-11	19-14
Minnesota	6-12	13-15
Wisconsin	5-13	14-14
Northwestern	2-16	6-22

	East Coast	
	Conference record	Overall record
Bucknell	10-4	19-10
Lafayette	8-6	15-13
Drexel	8-6	10-18
Rider	7-7	14-15
Delaware	7-7	12-16
Lehigh	6-8	12-19
Hofstra	5-9	14-15
Towson	5-9	6-22
Tournament: Lehigh over Bucknell, 76-74 (OT)		

	ECAC Metro	
	Conference record	Overall record
Marist	11-3	17-12
Fairleigh Dickinson	10-4	21-10
Long Island	9-5	15-13
Loyola (MD)	8-6	16-14
Saint Francis (PA)	6-8	9-19
Wagner	5-9	11-17
Robert Morris	4-10	9-19
St. Francis (NY)	3-11	7-21
Tournament: Fairleigh Dickinson over Loyola (MD), 63-59		

	ECAC NAC	
	Conference record	Overall record
Northeastern	13-3	22-9
Canisius	13-3	20-10
Siena	12-4	22-7
Niagara	11-5	16-12
Boston	9-7	15-15
Maine	5-11	11-17
Vermont	5-11	9-19
New Hampshire	4-12	7-22
Colgate	0-16	5-21
Hartford	--	7-21
Tournament: Northeastern over Boston, 68-67		

	ECAC South	
	Conference record	Overall record
Navy	11-3	26-6
Richmond	11-3	21-11
George Mason	10-4	18-11
William and Mary	9-5	16-12
James Madison	7-7	14-14
UNC Wilmington	4-10	12-16
American	3-11	9-19
East Carolina	1-13	7-21
Tournament: Navy over Richmond, 85-76		

	Gulf Star	
	Conference record	Overall record
Southeastern Louisiana	9-1	18-9
Nicholls State	6-4	17-10
Sam Houston State	5-4	16-12
Stephen F. Austin	4-5	16-10
Texas State	2-8	6-20
Northwestern State (LA)	2-8	3-25

	Ivy	
	Conference record	Overall record
Pennsylvania	10-4	13-14
Columbia	9-5	13-13
Cornell	8-6	14-12
Harvard	7-7	15-9
Yale	7-7	14-12
Princeton	7-7	11-15
Brown	5-9	9-18
Dartmouth	3-11	5-21

	Metro	
	Conference record	Overall record
Memphis State	13-1	31-4
Virginia Tech	10-4	20-9
Cincinnati	8-6	17-14
South Carolina	6-8	15-13
Tulane	6-8	15-13
Louisville	6-8	19-18
Florida State	4-10	14-16
Southern Mississippi	3-11	7-21
Tournament: Memphis State over Florida State, 90-86 (OT)		

	Metro Atlantic	
	Conference record	Overall record
Iona	11-3	26-5
Fordham	9-5	19-12
La Salle	8-6	15-13
Holy Cross	8-6	9-19
Army	7-7	16-13
Saint Peter's	5-9	15-14
Manhattan	4-10	8-20
Fairfield	4-10	11-17
Tournament: Iona over Fordham, 57-54		

	Mid-American	
	Conference record	Overall record
Ohio	14-4	22-8
Miami (OH)	13-5	20-11
Toledo	11-7	16-12
Kent State	11-7	17-13
Eastern Michigan	9-9	15-13
Ball State	8-10	13-16
Western Michigan	7-11	12-16
Northern Illinois	7-11	11-16
Bowling Green	6-12	12-15
Central Michigan	4-14	9-18
Tournament: Ohio over Miami (OH), 74-64		

	MEAC	
	Conference record	Overall record
North Carolina A&T	10-2	19-10
Howard	9-3	16-12
Delaware State	7-4	12-17
South Carolina State	7-4	11-16
Bethune-Cookman	4-6	8-19
Maryland-Eastern Shore	2-10	3-25
Morgan State	1-11	3-25
Tournament: North Carolina A&T over Howard, 71-69		

	Midwestern City	
	Conference record	Overall record
Loyola (IL)	13-1	27-6
Butler	9-5	19-10
Oral Roberts	8-6	15-15
Detroit	8-6	16-12
Xavier	7-7	16-13
Saint Louis	6-8	13-15
Evansville	4-10	13-16
Oklahoma City	1-13	6-20
Tournament: Loyola (IL) over Oral Roberts, 89-83		

	Missouri Valley	
	Conference record	Overall record
Tulsa	12-4	23-8
Illinois State	11-5	22-8
Wichita State	11-5	18-13
Creighton	9-7	20-12
Bradley	9-7	17-13
Southern Illinois	6-10	14-14
Indiana State	6-10	14-15
Drake	4-12	12-15
West Texas	4-12	11-17
Tournament: Wichita State over Tulsa, 84-82		

	Ohio Valley	
	Conference record	Overall record
Tennessee Tech	11-3	19-9
Youngstown State	9-5	19-11
Eastern Kentucky	9-5	16-13
Murray State	8-6	19-9
Middle Tennessee State	7-7	17-14
Akron	6-8	12-14
Austin Peay	4-10	8-19
Morehead State	2-12	7-20
Tournament: Middle Tennessee State over Youngstown State, 66-63		

	PCAA	
	Conference record	Overall record
UNLV	17-1	28-4
Fresno State	15-3	23-9
Cal State Fullerton	11-7	17-13
Utah State	10-8	17-11
San Jose State	10-8	16-13
UC Irvine	8-10	13-17
UC Santa Barbara	8-10	12-16
Pacific	5-13	9-19
New Mexico State	4-14	7-20
Long Beach State	2-16	4-23
Tournament: UNLV over Cal State Fullerton, 79-61		

	Pac-10	
	Conference record	Overall record
Washington	13-5	22-10
USC	13-5	19-10
Oregon State	12-6	22-9
Arizona	12-6	21-10
UCLA	12-6	21-12
Oregon	8-10	15-16
Arizona State	7-11	12-16
California	5-13	13-15
Washington State	5-13	13-15
Stanford	3-15	11-17

	SEC	
	Conference record	Overall record
LSU	13-5	19-10
Georgia	12-6	22-9
Alabama	11-7	23-10
Kentucky	11-7	18-13
Florida	9-9	18-12
Mississippi State	9-9	13-15
Auburn	8-10	22-12
Tennessee	8-10	22-15
Mississippi	5-13	11-17
Vanderbilt	4-14	11-17
Tournament: Auburn over Alabama, 53-49 (OT)		

	Southern	
	Conference record	Overall record
Chattanooga	14-2	24-8
Marshall	12-4	21-13
The Citadel	11-5	18-11
Western Carolina	8-8	14-14
VMI	7-9	16-14
Appalachian State	7-9	14-14
Davidson	6-10	10-20
Furman	4-12	7-21
East Tennessee State	3-13	9-18
Tournament: Marshall over VMI, 70-65		

	Southland	
	Conference record	Overall record
Louisiana Tech	11-1	29-3
McNeese State	9-3	18-10
Lamar	8-4	20-12
Arkansas State	6-6	14-14
Louisiana-Monroe	4-8	17-12
Texas-Arlington	3-9	12-16
North Texas	1-11	5-23
Tournament: Louisiana Tech over Lamar, 70-69		

	Southwest	
	Conference record	Overall record
Texas Tech	12-4	23-8
SMU	10-6	23-10
Texas A&M	10-6	19-11
Arkansas	10-6	22-13
TCU	8-8	16-12
Houston	8-8	16-14
Texas	7-9	15-13
Baylor	4-12	11-17
Rice	3-13	11-16
Tournament: Texas Tech over Arkansas, 67-64		

	SWAC	
	Conference record	Overall record
Alcorn State	13-1	23-7
Southern	9-5	19-11
Mississippi Valley State	7-7	18-11
Alabama State	7-7	14-17
Texas Southern	6-8	11-17
Jackson State	6-8	10-16
Grambling	4-10	8-19
Prairie View A&M	4-10	5-22
Tournament: Southern over Alcorn State, 85-70		

	Sun Belt	
	Conference record	Overall record
Virginia Commonwealth	12-2	26-6
Alabama-Birmingham	11-3	25-9
Old Dominion	9-5	19-12
South Florida	6-8	18-12
South Alabama	6-8	15-13
Jacksonville	6-8	15-14
Western Kentucky	5-9	14-14
Charlotte	1-13	5-23
Tournament: Virginia Commonwealth over Old Dominion, 87-82		

	TAAC	
	Conference record	Overall record
Georgia Southern	11-3	24-5
Mercer	10-4	22-9
Houston Baptist	10-4	21-8
Arkansas-Little Rock	9-5	17-13
Samford	7-7	18-12
Hardin-Simmons	7-7	11-17
Centenary	2-12	7-21
Georgia State	0-14	2-26
Tournament: Mercer over Arkansas-Little Rock, 105-96		

	WCAC	
	Conference record	Overall record
Pepperdine	11-1	23-9
Santa Clara	9-3	20-9
Saint Mary's (CA)	7-5	15-12
San Diego	5-7	16-11
Gonzaga	4-8	15-13
Portland	3-9	14-14
Loyola Marymount	3-9	11-16

	WAC	
	Conference record	Overall record
UTEP	12-4	22-10
San Diego State	11-5	23-8
Colorado State	9-7	18-12
New Mexico	9-7	19-13
BYU	9-7	15-14
Utah	8-8	15-16
Wyoming	7-9	15-14
Hawaii	5-11	10-18
Air Force	2-14	8-20
Tournament: San Diego State over UTEP, 87-81		

	Independents
	Overall record
Notre Dame	21-9
Dayton	19-10
DePaul	19-10
Marquette	20-11
Texas-San Antonio	18-10
Chicago State	16-11
Radford	16-12
Utica	15-12
Louisiana-Lafayette	17-14
Brooklyn	15-13
Charleston Southern	13-15
Eastern Washington	12-15
Monmouth	12-15
Stetson	12-16
Texas-Pan American	12-16
New Orleans	11-19
Florida A&M	10-18
Central Florida	10-18
Tennessee State	9-19
Augusta	8-20
Campbell	5-22
U.S. International	1-27

1985 NCAA Tournament Players
Selected in 1985 NBA Draft

Round 1

1. New York Knicks – Patrick Ewing, Georgetown
2. Indiana Pacers – Wayman Tisdale, Oklahoma
4. Seattle Supersonics – Xavier McDaniel, Wichita State
5. Atlanta Hawks – Jon Koncak, SMU
6. Sacramento Kings – Joe Kleine, Arkansas
7. Golden State Warriors – Chris Mullin, St. John's
8. Dallas Mavericks – Detlef Schrempf, Washington
10. Phoenix Suns – Ed Pinckney, Villanova
11. Chicago Bulls – Keith Lee, Memphis State
13. Utah Jazz – Karl Malone, Louisiana Tech
14. San Antonio Sputs – Alfredrick Hughes, Loyola (IL)
16. Dallas Mavericks – Bill Wennington, St. John's
19. Houston Rockets – Steve Harris, Tulsa
20. Boston Celtics – Sam Vincent, Michigan State
22. Milwaukee Bucks – Jerry Reynolds, LSU
23. Los Angeles Lakers – A.C. Green, Oregon State

Round 2

26. Indiana Pacers – Bill Martin, Georgetown
27. Indiana Pacers – Dwayne McClain, Villanova
28. Chicago Bulls – Ken Johnson, Michigan State
33. Philadelphia 76ers – Greg Stokes, Iowa
34. Chicago Bulls – Aubrey Sherrod, Wichita State
35. San Antonio Spurs – Tyrone Corbin, DePaul
36. New Jersey Nets – Yvon Joseph, Georgia Tech
39. Portland Trailblazers – George Montgomery, Illinois
41. Atlanta Hawks – Lorenzo Charles, North Carolina State
42. Golden State Warriors – Bobby Lee Hurt, Alabama
43. Denver Nuggets – Barry Stevens, Iowa State
46. Chicago Bulls – Adrian Branch, Maryland

Round 3

48. Indiana Pacers – Kenny Patterson, DePaul
53. Seattle Supersonics – Rolando Lamb, Virginia Commonwealth
55. Cleveland Cavaliers – Herb Johnson, Tulsa
57. Houston Rockets – Michael Payne, Iowa

59. Atlanta Hawks – Sedric Toney, Dayton

61. Portland Trailblazers – Perry Young, Virginia Tech

66. Sacramento Kings – Michael Adams, Boston College

70. Boston Celtics – Andre Battle, Loyola (IL)

Round 4

71. Golden State Warriors – Luster Goodwin, UTEP

76. Sacramento Kings – Willie Simmons, Louisiana Tech

78. Phoenix Suns – Granger Hall, Temple

79. Cleveland Cavaliers – Mark Davis, Old Dominion

81. Washington Bullets – Richie Adams, UNLV

86. Dallas Mavericks – Bubba Jennings, Texas Tech

87. Detroit Pistons – Spud Webb, North Carolina State

89. Denver Nuggets – Pete Williams, Arizona

91. Milwaukee Bucks – Cozell McQueen, North Carolina State

Round 5

96. New York Knicks – Mike Schlegel, Virginia Commonwealth

97. Seattle Supersonics – Lou Stefanovic, Illinois State

99. Los Angeles Clippers – Wayne Carlander, USC

106. San Antonio Spurs – Clayton Olivier, USC

113. Philadelphia 76ers – Carl Wright, SMU

Round 6

117. Golden State Warriors – Gerald Crosby, Georgia

118. Indiana Pacers – Stu Primus, Boston College

119. New York Knicks – Kent Lockhart, UTEP

120. Sacramento Kings – Charles Valentine, Arkansas

124. Phoenix Suns – Charles Rayne, Temple

125. Cleveland Cavaliers – Ricky Johnson, Illinois State

126. Chicago Bulls – Dan Meagher, Duke

137. Milwaukee Bucks – Quentin Anderson, Texas Tech

Round 7

147. Cleveland Cavaliers – Buzz Peterson, North Carolina

149. Chicago Bulls – Jeff Adkins, Maryland

152. San Antonio Spurs – Al Young, Virginia Tech

154. New Jersey Nets – Gary McLain, Villanova

155. Dallas Mavericks – Ed Catchings, UNLV

156. Detroit Pistons – Frank James, UNLV

157. Indiana Pacers – Don Turney, Marshall
158. Denver Nuggets – Eddie Smith, Arizona

1985 Men's NCAA Basketball Tournament

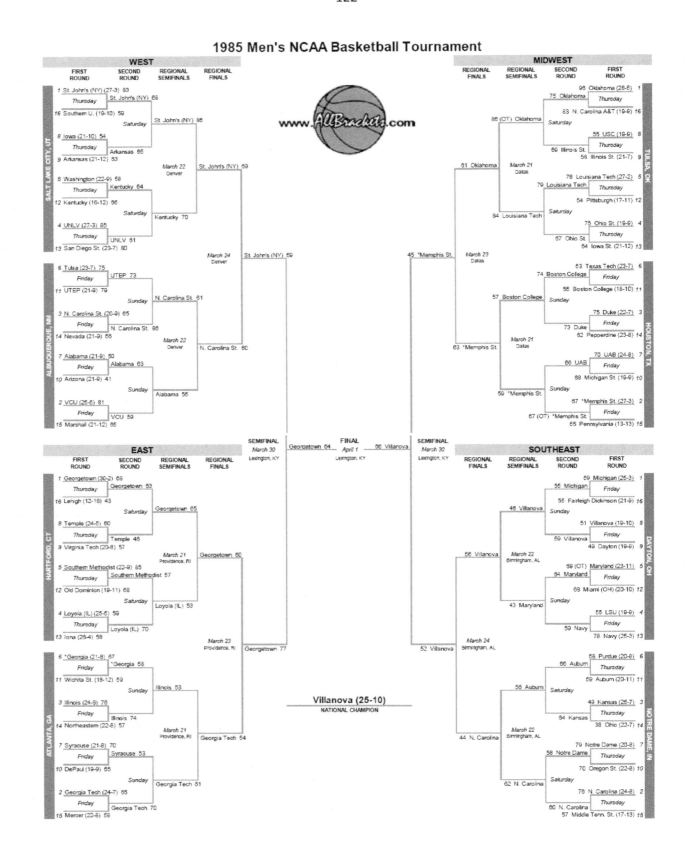

WEST

FIRST ROUND	SECOND ROUND	REGIONAL SEMIFINALS	REGIONAL FINALS

SALT LAKE CITY, UT

1 St. John's (NY) (27-3) 83
Thursday
St. John's (NY) 66
16 Southern U. (19-10) 59
St. John's (NY) 86
Saturday
8 Iowa (21-10) 54
Thursday
Arkansas 65
9 Arkansas (21-12) 63
St. John's (NY) 69
March 22 Denver
5 Washington (22-9) 58
Thursday
Kentucky 64
12 Kentucky (16-12) 66
Kentucky 70
Saturday
4 UNLV (27-3) 85
Thursday
UNLV 61
13 San Diego St. (23-7) 80

St. John's (NY) 59
March 24 Denver

ALBUQUERQUE, NM

6 Tulsa (23-7) 75
Friday
UTEP 73
11 UTEP (21-9) 79
N. Carolina St. 61
Sunday
3 N. Carolina St. (20-9) 65
Friday
N. Carolina St. 86
14 Nevada (21-9) 56
N. Carolina St. 60
March 22 Denver
7 Alabama (21-9) 50
Friday
Alabama 63
10 Arizona (21-9) 41
Alabama 55
Sunday
2 VCU (25-6) 81
Friday
VCU 59
15 Marshall (21-12) 65

MIDWEST

REGIONAL FINALS	REGIONAL SEMIFINALS	SECOND ROUND	FIRST ROUND

TULSA, OK

96 Oklahoma (28-5) 1
Oklahoma 75
Thursday
83 N. Carolina A&T (19-9) 16
Oklahoma 86 (OT)
Saturday
55 USC (19-9) 8
Illinois St. 69
Thursday
58 Illinois St. (21-7) 9
Oklahoma 81
March 21 Dallas
78 Louisiana Tech (27-2) 5
Louisiana Tech 79
Thursday
54 Pittsburgh (17-11) 12
Louisiana Tech 84
Saturday
75 Ohio St. (19-9) 4
Ohio St. 67
Thursday
64 Iowa St. (21-12) 13

*Memphis St. 45
March 23 Dallas

HOUSTON, TX

53 Texas Tech (23-7) 6
Boston College 74
Friday
55 Boston College (18-10) 11
Boston College 57
Sunday
75 Duke (22-7) 3
Duke 73
Friday
62 Pepperdine (23-8) 14
*Memphis St. 63
March 21 Dallas
70 UAB (24-8) 7
UAB 66
Friday
68 Michigan St. (19-9) 10
*Memphis St. 59
Sunday
67 *Memphis St. (27-3) 2
*Memphis St. 67 (OT)
Friday
65 Pennsylvania (13-13) 15

SEMIFINAL	FINAL	SEMIFINAL
March 30 Lexington, KY	*April 1 Lexington, KY*	*March 30 Lexington, KY*

Georgetown 64 — 66 Villanova

EAST

FIRST ROUND	SECOND ROUND	REGIONAL SEMIFINALS	REGIONAL FINALS

HARTFORD, CT

1 Georgetown (30-2) 68
Thursday
Georgetown 63
16 Lehigh (12-19) 43
Georgetown 65
Saturday
8 Temple (24-5) 60
Thursday
Temple 46
9 Virginia Tech (20-8) 57
Georgetown 60
March 21 Providence, RI
5 Southern Methodist (22-9) 85
Thursday
Southern Methodist 57
12 Old Dominion (19-11) 68
Loyola (IL) 53
Saturday
4 Loyola (IL) (25-5) 59
Thursday
Loyola (IL) 70
13 Iona (26-4) 58

Georgetown 77
March 23 Providence, RI

ATLANTA, GA

6 *Georgia (21-9) 67
Friday
*Georgia 56
11 Wichita St. (18-12) 59
Illinois 53
Sunday
3 Illinois (24-8) 76
Friday
Illinois 74
14 Northeastern (22-8) 57
Georgia Tech 54
March 21 Providence, RI
7 Syracuse (21-8) 70
Friday
Syracuse 53
10 DePaul (19-9) 65
Georgia Tech 61
Sunday
2 Georgia Tech (24-7) 65
Friday
Georgia Tech 70
15 Mercer (22-8) 58

Villanova (25-10)
NATIONAL CHAMPION

SOUTHEAST

REGIONAL FINALS	REGIONAL SEMIFINALS	SECOND ROUND	FIRST ROUND

DAYTON, OH

59 Michigan (25-3) 1
Michigan 55
Friday
55 Fairleigh Dickinson (21-9) 16
Villanova 46
Sunday
51 Villanova (19-10) 8
Villanova 59
Friday
49 Dayton (19-9) 9
Villanova 55
March 22 Birmingham, AL
69 Maryland (23-11) 5
Maryland 64 (OT)
Friday
68 Miami (OH) (20-10) 12
Maryland 43
Sunday
55 LSU (19-9) 4
Navy 59
Friday
78 Navy (25-3) 13

Villanova 52
March 24 Birmingham, AL

NOTRE DAME, IN

58 Purdue (20-8) 6
Auburn 66
Thursday
59 Auburn (20-11) 11
Auburn 56
Saturday
49 Kansas (26-7) 3
Kansas 64
Thursday
38 Ohio (22-7) 14
N. Carolina 44
March 22 Birmingham, AL
79 Notre Dame (20-8) 7
Notre Dame 58
Thursday
70 Oregon St. (22-8) 10
N. Carolina 62
Sunday
76 N. Carolina (24-8) 2
N. Carolina 60
Thursday
57 Middle Tenn. St. (17-13) 15

Made in the USA
Middletown, DE
12 December 2019